Contents

1	Acknowledgments
3	Foreword
4	Executive Summary
5	Part I: Nine Essential Tasks for Creating a Diversity and Inclusion Strategic Plan: A Structured Approach and Key Resources

Essential Task 1: Solicit buy-in and commitment from key stakeholders

Essential Task 2: Build a strong foundation for the initiative by assessing the existing landscape

Essential Task 3: Identify leverage points and challenges

Essential Task 4: Set diversity and inclusion goals that align with organization mission, vision, and values

Essential Task 5: Set clear and realistic objectives, supporting tasks, and action steps required to achieve goals

Essential Task 6: Develop accountability methods and metrics to measure achievement of each objective

Essential Task 7: Establish roles, responsibilities, and decision-making channels

Essential Task 8: Develop a realistic timeline for executing all action steps

Essential Task 9: Prepare the written plan

| 21 | Part II: Strategies to Meet Diversity and Inclusion Goals |
| 57 | Part III: References and Resources |

...ublication of the Association of American Medical Colleges. The AAMC serves and leads the academic medicine community to
...ne health of all. www.aamc.org.

First edition published 2014. Second edition 2016.

ISBN-13: 978-1523815890

Diversity and Inclusion in Academic Medicine: A Strategic Planning Guide

Acknowledgments

The AAMC extends its appreciation to all of the following groups who participated in writing and reviewing the content for this guide.

Group on Diversity and Inclusion (GDI) Diversity Strategic Planning Working Group

Under the leadership of GDI Chair David A. Acosta, MD, FAAFP, and GDI Chair-elect Leon McDougle, MD, MPH, the GDI Steering Committee appointed the GDI Diversity Strategic Planning Working Group. The charter states:

> The GDI Diversity Strategic Planning Working Group will develop a strategic plan template for GDI members that will help build their capacity for integrating new or existing diversity and inclusion initiatives within their institutions.

> The GDI Diversity Strategic Planning Working Group will be chaired by Maria Soto-Greene, MD, and GDI representatives from each region who have the expertise shall be appointed to this working group.

The following are GDI Diversity Strategic Planning Working Group members who developed the content for this guide:

- Maria L. Soto-Greene, MD, Chair, Rutgers New Jersey Medical School (formerly UMDNJ-New Jersey Medical School)
- Juan Amador, Director and GDI Program Leader, AAMC
- Cynthia Boyd, MD, MBA, Rush Medical College of Rush University Medical Center
- André L. Churchwell, MD, Vanderbilt University School of Medicine
- Sunny Gibson, MSW, Northwestern University The Feinberg School of Medicine
- Renee Navarro, MD, University of California, San Francisco, School of Medicine
- Ann-Christine Nyquist, MD, MSPH, University of Colorado School of Medicine
- Dominga Padilla, MD, Rutgers New Jersey Medical School (formerly UMDNJ-New Jersey Medical School)
- Deborah Plummer, PhD, University of Massachusetts Medical School
- Tony Rodriguez, MD, Drexel University College of Medicine
- Valerie Romero-Leggott, MD, University of New Mexico Health Sciences Center

Group on Diversity and Inclusion (GDI) and Group on Institutional Planning (GIP) Toolkit Working Group

In 2015, under the leadership of GDI Chair Joan Y. Reede, MD, MPH, MS, MBA, and GDI Chair-elect Edward J. Callahan, PhD, the GDI Steering Committee collaborated with the GIP Steering Committee to appoint the GDI/GIP Toolkit Advisory Working Group. The charge of the working group states:

> This advisory working group, which comprises three members of the Group on Diversity and Inclusion (GDI) and three members of the Group on Institutional Planning (GIP), is charged with assisting and advising on the creation of a Web-based toolkit to accompany the *Diversity and Inclusion in Academic Medicine:*

Acknowledgments

A Strategic Planning Guide publication. The Web-based toolkit is designed to accompany the guide and provide additional resources and sample documents to help in creating a diversity and inclusion strategic plan.

The GDI/GIP Toolkit Advisory Working Group members who developed the content for this Web-based toolkit, as well as updates to the original strategic planning guide, include the following:

- Lynn Gordon, MD, PhD, David Geffen School of Medicine at UCLA
- Basma Selim, PhD, University of Central Florida College of Medicine
- David McIntosh, PhD, University of Louisville School of Medicine
- Karen Smith, Washington University in St. Louis School of Medicine
- Deborah L. Plummer, PhD, University of Massachusetts Medical School
- Elaine Van der Put, PhD, MSPH, University of Miami Leonard M. Miller School of Medicine

2013 Diversity and Inclusion Forum

The diversity and inclusion innovation forum annually convenes a group of thought leaders on a diversity, inclusion, or health equity topic of interest to the broader academic medicine community. The 2013 forum topic was diversity strategic planning. For this project, the AAMC collaborated with GDI members to create a publication that will guide institutions seeking to integrate diversity, inclusion, and health equity goals into their strategic planning process.

Group on Student Affairs Committee on Student Diversity Affairs (GSA-COSDA)

The student diversity section of this resource was developed by Sunny Gibson, MSW; GSA-COSDA Chair Wanda Lipscomb, PhD; and AAMC Senior Specialist Lisa J. Jennings, MA, MEd.

GDI Steering Committee

GDI Steering Committee members reviewed, contributed to, and approved the development of this guide. A special thank you to David A. Acosta, MD, FAAFP, University of California Davis Health System, and Leon McDougle, MD, MPH, The Ohio State University Wexner Medical Center, for their significant contributions in reviewing and editing this guide.

AAMC Staff

Juan Amador, Director and Group Program Leader

Taniecea Arceneaux, PhD, Senior Diversity Research Specialist

Laura Castillo-Page, PhD, Senior Director, Diversity Policy and Programs and Organizational Capacity Building Portfolio

Katie Hunter, Administrative Specialist

Angela R. Moses, Senior Program Specialist

Marc A. Nivet, EdD, MBA, Chief Diversity Officer

Tiffani St. Cloud, Director of Educational Initiatives

Heather Sacks, Director, Planning and Administrative Affairs

Michelle Shader, Learning Design Manager

Jessica Vaughan, Organizational Capacity Building Portfolio Coordinator

Foreword

It is both an exciting and challenging time for diversity in academic medicine. A growing appreciation for diversity and inclusion as drivers of excellence is coupled with the charge of building and sustaining the capacity to positively affect health care for all. Within this environment of change, we turn to you, the leaders of our medical schools and teaching hospitals, to position your own institutions toward realizing these important goals.

Your role as a diversity leader in academic medicine is critical to our success in achieving the tripartite mission. Many of you have already made great strides in implementing successful initiatives to support and foster underrepresented students and faculty, and the time has come to build upon that progress. There is no question that the accreditation elements (formerly standards) of the Liaison Committee on Medical Education are an important mechanism for assessing institutional climate and culture. However, an even more salient motivator for change is the institutional excellence that follows when acknowledging diversity as a strategic imperative.

This guide and the associated toolkit, produced by a multidisciplinary team of experts, provide a roadmap that will not only help you comply with important diversity standards, but also pave the way for developing and sustaining a culture of inclusion at your institutions. We share with you these valuable resources, which will ensure that you are well-equipped to continue on this journey toward excellence.

Marc Nivet, EdD, MBA
Chief Diversity Officer
Association of American Medical Colleges

Executive Summary

This guide and toolkit provide assistance for institutions at varying points on the diversity and inclusion continuum and in their strategic planning process. These resources will help to optimize organizational culture and health care outcomes at all academic health centers and assist with implementing the Liaison Committee on Medical Education accreditation elements (formerly standards). It is important to note that plans for diversity and inclusion should be part of and central to overall strategic planning of the AAMC-member institution.

This guide is organized in three sections:

I. **Nine Essential Tasks for Creating a Diversity and Inclusion Strategy Plan.** This first section is for those who are in the earliest planning stage. Each essential task and the supplemental tools associated with the task create a roadmap for the process of strategic planning. Although you should work through the tasks in order, you will find that strategic planning can be a circular process. As you conduct research and refine your thinking, you may return to earlier tasks to amend and/or expand your original thinking. Treat this as a flexible, rather than rigid, process.

II. **Strategies to Meet Diversity and Inclusion Goals.** This second section expands on the nine essential tasks by offering specific strategies and resources for developing strategies, including why diversity belongs in a plan, the role of the diversity officer in the process, and methods for achieving diversity and inclusion at every level of an institution.

III. **References.** This section provides comprehensive references for further exploration.

Part I

Nine Essential Tasks for Creating a Diversity and Inclusion

The process of preparing a diversity and inclusion strategic plan is complex and labor-intensive. The nine essential tasks outlined here are intended to offer structure to the process and make it more manageable and productive. Each task comprises a task summary, key questions to answer, tips to ensure that task completion is successful, and selected resources to provide more information.

Getting Ready

Before you begin working on the essential tasks outlined in this guide, please see the Getting Ready page of the toolkit. This resource will help you do the following:

- Assemble your team
- Establish scope
- Determine your timeline

How to Access the Toolkit

To get started, go to **www.aamc.org/diversitystrategicplanning**. All tools, resources, and downloadable documents are available there.

Essential Task 1: Solicit buy-in and commitment from key stakeholders

Task Summary: This is the initial task but also one that underpins many other tasks you will complete as you create and implement your plan. Given the nature of diversity, your strategic plan will touch every person at an institution; therefore, at every step, you will need to find allies and create partnerships to ensure the plan is carried out. The first step is essential because the task that follows it assesses where you are currently, which requires the permission and assistance of many across the organization.

Method: Answer the questions that follow (Stakeholder Identification template available in the toolkit).

a) Who asked you to develop a diversity strategic plan and why?

b) How much support (advocacy, financial, personnel, protected time, etc.) can you count on to help make your plan a reality in the long term?

c) What other stakeholders need to be involved to assess where you are currently and implement your proposed strategic priorities in the future?

d) Who are other champions, leaders, and allies who can move the strategic plan along?

e) Which groups are more interested and which are less interested in cultural change? See Diversity Adoption and Engagement Resource page for guidance on managing diversity culture change.

Tips

- Never underestimate the value of allies. There are many people in your organization already working on the assessments and strategic priorities you will create in this process.

- Always tailor your message to the audience; it should always be about how diversity can help them reach their goals.

- All resources below are available in the toolkit. Please see page 5 for link to toolkit.

Communication Resources

- The Case for Diversity and Inclusion and the Role of Diversity Officers in Part II of the *Strategic Planning Guide*

- Elevator Speech: Tips and Samples

- Diversity Rationale: University of Louisville School of Medicine

- Diversity Statement: University of Massachusetts Medical School

- AAMC Communicating Your Strategic Plan Teleconference

- AAMC Diversity 3.0 Learning Series Webinar, The Difference: How the Power of Diversity Creates Better Groups, Firms, Schools, and Societies

Strategic Planning Resources

- AAMC Diversity and Inclusion in Academic Medicine: A Strategic Planning Guide Webinar

- AAMC GDI Navigator to Excellence: Strategic Planning Webinar

- AAMC Introduction to Strategic Planning

- AAMC Organizational Alignment Presentation

Diversity Resources

- Diversity Adoption and Engagement Resource (Loden M. 1995. Implementing Diversity: Best Practices for Making Diversity Work in Your Organization. New York: McGraw-Hill).

- Smith DG. 2009. Diversity's Promise for Higher Education: Making It Work. Baltimore, MD: Johns Hopkins University Press. ISBN: 1421405733.

- Ross HJ. 2011. ReInventing Diversity: Transforming Organizational Community to Strengthen People, Purpose, and Performance. Lanham, MD: Rowan & Littlefield. ISBN: 9781442210431.

Essential Task 2: Build a strong foundation for the initiative by assessing the existing landscape

Task Summary: Strategic planning begins with an assessment of where your institution is on the diversity and inclusion continuum, which refers to the stages of diversity delineated by Marc Nivet, the AAMC's chief diversity officer, in *Diversity 3.0: A Necessary Systems Upgrade.*[1] This effort will provide insight into potential challenges and leverage points (see Essential Task 3). Fortunately, there are a number of institutional readiness checklists to aid in the process (see resources below).

Method: Answer the questions that follow (Assess the Existing Landscape template available in the toolkit).

a) How have commitment and action around diversity and inclusion evolved over time? What, if any, seminal events need to be considered?

b) Where was the focus on diversity five years ago? Where is it now?

c) What policies are already in place to support diversity and inclusion? The difference between policy and practice can sometimes be dramatic. Things are often done in a certain way because "that's the way they have always been done." The impact on processes such as hiring, recruitment, retention, professional development, lab space, support staff, promotion, and merit raises can be profound.

Consider policy versus practice in the following:

- Hiring practices
- Recruitment
- Equity (compensation, access, promotion, treatment, etc.)
- Mentoring

d) What are the particular imperatives driving diversity and inclusion strategic planning within your institution? Are there any state laws, community efforts, or institutional mandates that create pressure points and opportunities?

e) What have previous climate assessments told you about the environment?

f) What other sources of data can you access to assess the organizational culture (e.g., exit survey data, nonmatriculating student survey data)?

g) What was done with the data that were previously gathered? How were the data used to inform practice? Are any of the data/analyses still relevant?

Tips

- Use checklists to assess readiness—there is no need to reinvent the wheel.
- Make your plan broad enough so that it is a driver for institutional excellence.
- All resources below are available in the toolkit. Please see page 5 for link to toolkit.

Organizational Assessment Resources

- Getting Ready: Data Collection Self-Assessment
- National Multicultural Institute, Identifying Organizational Readiness Checklist
- University of Washington School of Medicine, Board of Deans Report Checklist
- Organizational Readiness: HR Questions

Climate and Culture Resources

- Assessing the Existing Landscape in Part II of the *Strategic Planning Guide*
- AAMC Diversity Engagement Survey
- AAMC Assessing Institutional Climate and Culture Webcast

AAMC Data Resources

- Data and Analysis
- Facts and Figures Data Series

Make your plan broad
enough so that it is a driver
for institutional excellence.

Essential Task 3: Identify leverage points and challenges

Task Summary: Your efforts will be more fruitful if you identify the leverage points that already exist within your institution. Leverage is often tied to urgent initiatives and concerns. Likewise, if you know what challenges already exist, you can build strategies to address them and ensure that momentum is not lost.

Method: Answer the questions that follow (Leverage Points, Challenges, and SWOT Analysis template available in the toolkit).

a) Outline your organizational readiness. How can you control and define your pace, flow, and momentum?

b) How committed are constituents to embracing an agenda that supports progressive change and equality for all members of the community, regardless of identity characteristics? (See Diversity Adoption and Engagement Resource in Task 1 for information on how to engage people across the adoption continuum.)

c) Shift the organizational mindset. Define urgency for your institution. What is your "burning platform"? Consider the following:

-   Numbers

-   Culture

-   Turnover

d) Determine the baseline of financial and human capital resources that supports diversity and inclusion integration at your institution. What are the current programs? Where are they located? How does diversity planning fit into the overall financial plan of the institution?

e) Have you educated yourself about the change-management process involved in this effort? Where is your organization in the process? What can you reasonably expect to accomplish in the coming months to move the organization forward? (See works by Loden and Kotter listed under Organizational Change Resources for more information on change management.)

How can you create urgency?

Tips

-   Recognize the leverage points available to you, such as the Liaison Committee on Medical Education (LCME) accreditation elements (formerly standards), Accreditation Council for Graduate Medical Education (ACGME) core competencies, and new National Standards for Culturally and Linguistically Appropriate Services. Learn to translate the standards into meaningful language that will have the impact you need on the issues that are important to your administration.

-   Focus on quantitative and qualitative data to validate your goals.

-   Understand that all key leadership must know the vision and deliver the same message throughout the organization on a consistent basis.

-   Realize that diversity initiatives go hand-in-hand with organizational change; therefore, expect challenges to the concept and your authority.

-   Be aware that diversity and inclusion initiatives can fail if the institution has not invested in the human capital to do the work. Having enough of the right people on board with expertise and skills is important to doing the work efficiently and correctly.

-   All resources below are available in the toolkit. Please see page 5 for link to toolkit.

Data Collection Standards

- LCME Data Collection Instrument Survey, Sections 3.3 and 7.6
- U.S. Department of Health and Human Services, National Standards for Culturally and Linguistically Appropriate Services in Health Care

AAMC Data Resources

- Request AAMC Data
- Faculty Forward Engagement Survey
- Diversity Engagement Survey

Organizational Change Resources

- Achieving Diversity and Inclusion in Part II of the *Strategic Planning Guide*
- Loden M. 1995. Implementing Diversity: Best Practices for Making Diversity Work in Your Organization. New York: McGraw-Hill.
- Kotter International. 2014. The 8-step process for leading change.

Essential Task 4: Set diversity and inclusion goals that align with organization mission, vision, and values

Task Summary: Your goals for diversity and inclusion reflect the desired outcomes of the strategic plan. To achieve them, they must align with the institution's stated mission, vision, and values and be seen by all as strategic initiatives so they are not "siloed."

Method: Answer the questions that follow.

1) Review and complete the Key Terms and Examples: Vision, Mission, and Values document found in the toolkit.

2) Answer the questions that follow (Goal Setting and Alignment template and Goal and Strategy template available in the toolkit).

   a) Based on the data you analyzed, what diversity and inclusion goals should your organization focus on? (Goals are the broad outcomes your plan seeks to achieve. For example, "Develop innovations in education to prepare students and trainees from diverse backgrounds to be collaborative practitioners of medicine.")

   b) What is the exact desired outcome for each goal? (Outcomes should be specific and measurable. For example, "Students will be able to describe a strategy for engaging medical practitioners from a variety of backgrounds.")

   c) To what extent are diversity and inclusion seen as strategic imperatives and part of everyone's responsibilities?

   - How are these imperatives communicated to the organization's broader community?

   - How well are these imperatives understood?

   d) If the diversity and inclusion imperatives are not well communicated or understood, answer the following questions:

   - What would be necessary to incorporate diversity and inclusion as strategic initiatives (e.g., getting buy-in and support from many levels of the organization, including, most importantly, senior leadership)?

   - How could you go about elevating the level of importance for these strategic initiatives?

   e) What immediate steps can you take to better incorporate diversity and inclusion within all missions of the institution?

   f) Is there a "charge" from senior leadership that reflects commitment and clear expectations? Identify one or more senior leaders who will be responsible for the diversity and inclusion strategic goals. (For example, if there is a financial goal, it might be assigned to the chief financial officer. If there is a curriculum change, this might be assign to the dean of medical students.)

Tips

- Prioritize goals.

- Explain goals clearly and in measurable terms so that metrics can be applied for assessment.

- Remember that the plan is not static and will define a long-term process that evolves with continuous effort from everyone within the institution.

- All resources below are available in the toolkit. Please see page 5 for link to toolkit.

Goal Setting Resources

- On Strategy, Goal Setting as an Art Form
- University of Wisconsin–Madison Project Prioritization Guide
- Victorian Department of Health (Australia), Writing Measurable Objectives (SMART Goals)
- Tarrant County College, Writing Outcomes/Objectives

Diversity Goals Examples

- Texas A&M Health Science Center College of Medicine

Strategic Planning Resources

- Society for College and University Planning, A Practical Guide to Strategic Planning in Higher Education
- U.S. Department of Energy Guidelines for Strategic Planning, Sections 2 and 4

What steps can you take
now to prevent diversity and
inclusion from being siloed?

Essential Task 5: Set clear and realistic objectives, supporting tasks, and action steps required to achieve goals

Task Summary: Achieving your goals requires a top-down, highly structured approach to the actual work that will be done by you and your committees. This task defines each step in the process.

Method

1) Review and complete the Key Terms and Examples: Goals, Objectives, Tasks, and Action Steps document found in the toolkit.

2) Answer the questions that follow (Goals, Objectives, Tasks, and Actions template and Goal and Strategy template available in the toolkit).

   a) What are your objectives for each goal? *(Objectives are the strategies to achieve each goal.)*

   b) What key tasks are necessary for each objective to be achieved? *(Tasks represent the work that must be assigned.)*

   c) What action steps are needed to complete each task? *(Action steps define the work flow.)*

Tips

- Establish two to four objectives per goal (recommended). However, some goals may take more than four objectives to implement.
- Prioritize the objectives.
- Take care to identify levels of complexity involved in each task and any challenges that may emerge. Seek input from those with knowledge of details.
- All resources below are available in the toolkit. Please see page 5 for link to toolkit.

Related Resources

- Achieving Diversity and Inclusion in Part II of the *Strategic Planning Guide*
- Bimbaum R. 1988. How Colleges Work: The Cybernetics of Academic Organization and Leadership. San Francisco, CA: Jossey-Bass.
- University of Texas Medical Branch Strategic Planning Process Diagram
- AAMC Group on Institutional Planning Strategic Planning Resources

> **Take care to identify levels of complexity involved in each task and any challenges that may emerge.**

Essential Task 6: Develop accountability methods and metrics to measure achievement of objectives

Task Summary: Metrics allow you to monitor your performance. Baseline assessments of where you are, followed by targeted goals, are important components of metric development. Accountability will keep momentum moving forward.

Note: The next three tasks address the development of processes and structures to ensure successful implementation of goals and objectives. Establishing metrics is one important process. Having an implementation plan that assigns each objective to an individual for completion within a specified time frame is another (see Tasks 7 and 8). Linking diversity and inclusion objectives to the annual budget and operating plans is yet another (Task 8). You will need to develop the processes that are appropriate for your institution.

Method

1) Review the Key Terms and Examples: Measure, Metrics, Target, and Benchmark document found in the toolkit.

2) Answer the questions that follow (Metric Development template and Goal and Strategy template available in the toolkit).

   a) Is each objective framed so that results have an associated metric (e.g., can you set a success measure for excellence in faculty diversity)?

   b) How will metrics be gathered, analyzed, and reported and with what frequency? The Data Dictionary template provides a place to record a definition, data source, and frequency for data collection on each metric.

   c) What baseline metrics are you going to use to gauge your success for each objective? When assessing metrics, it is useful to assess the following: (1) your organization's trend/baseline and (2) how your organization is doing compared with peers. Consider using data from the AAMC on specialties and ACGME data for national values. (See Data Collection and Accountability Resources below for resource links.)

   d) What is your target for performance going forward and to whom are you reporting your progress?

   e) How will you monitor accountability for each goal? Consider using multiple points of accountability throughout the institution (you do not want to put the total responsibility on senior leadership alone). Consider using dashboards for tracking and reporting progress on each goal.

   f) How will you know if the accountability process is sufficiently transparent?

Tips

- Performing an annual trend analysis of the data will provide insight into how well you are reaching your targeted objectives and goals.

- Ongoing reassessment will support sustainability and continuous improvement.

- All resources below are available in the toolkit. Please see page 5 for link to toolkit.

Data Collection and Accountability Resources

- Responsible Accountable Consult Inform (RACI) Charting
- Data Dictionary Template
- Performance Dashboard
- Person SD et al. 2015. Measuring diversity and inclusion in academic medicine: the diversity engagement survey. Academic Medicine 90(12):1675-1683.
- Brotherton SE, Etzel SI. 2014. Graduate medical education, 2013–2014. JAMA 312(22):2427-2445 (ACGME data source).
- AAMC Faculty Roster. Distribution of U.S. medical school faculty by sex, race/ethnicity, rank, and department.

Related Resources

- Assessing the Existing Landscape in Part II of the *Strategic Planning Guide*
- Workforce Diversity Network, Diversity Metrics, Measurement, and Evaluation

Metrics will allow you to monitor your performance.

Essential Task 7: Establish roles, responsibilities, and decision-making channels

Task Summary: Having the right people on board with the necessary skills and dedication is essential. An advisory council can be appointed, composed of people who represent a cross-section of the organization and key stakeholders. Individuals who will be responsible for and assist in implementation will need to be assigned to implementation teams. Communication and decision-making channels need to be very clear and agreed upon by all.

Method: Answer the questions that follow (Roles, Responsibilities, and Decision Making template available in the toolkit).

a) **Advisory council.** Who has the knowledge, skill, and commitment to work with you? Who are the key stakeholders and thought and opinion leaders from within and external to the organization? **Note:** You can use the Stakeholder Analysis grid in Task 1 to identify advisory council members.

b) **Implementation group.** Have you established mechanisms or structures to ensure the implementation of your plan and accountability? This information should be documented in a RACI chart (see Task 6).

c) **Implementation group.** Are the responsibilities of each role clearly defined, and are required tasks outlined in a way that can be implemented? Has protected time been allotted for work in this area? **Note:** Task assignments should be recorded on your Goal and Strategy template (Tasks 4–6).

d) What mechanisms do you have in place to communicate the strategic plan across the organization? Who needs to be involved to develop a communication plan?

- Who needs to see what level of detail?
- What do different audience segments need to know about the plan?

e) What kinds of communication challenges are typical within your organization, and how can you overcome them? (You might want to refer back to the communication elements you developed in Task 1.) **Note:** Your communication plan will not be implemented until the plan is written.

Tips

- Consider an advisory council to keep the institution focused, accountable, and on track. The council should comprise people who represent a cross-section of the organization and who are champions for the initiative.
- Plan to educate your team.
- Understand that the dean needs to hold the chairs accountable for their diversity efforts. You are not the "sheriff"; rather, you are the messenger.
- All resources below are available in the toolkit. Please see page 5 for link to toolkit.

Roles and Responsibilities Resources

- Joint Planning Diversity Functions Chart
- University of Massachusetts Medical School Diversity Initiative Organization Chart

Advisory Council and Communication Resources

- Developing an Effective Advisory Council
- Meeting Planning and Communication

Related Resources

- The Role of Diversity Officers in Part II of the *Strategic Planning Guide*
- National Multicultural Institute, Identify Organizational Readiness Checklist
- Plummer DL, ed. 2002. Handbook of Diversity Management: Beyond Awareness to Competency-Based Learning. Lanham, MD: University Press of America.
- Plummer DL, Jordan CG. 2007. Going plaid: integrating diversity into business strategy. OD Practitioner 39(2):35-40.
- Axelrod NR. 2004. Advisory Councils. Washington, DC: BoardSource.

Having the right people on board with the necessary skills and dedication is essential.

Essential Task 8: Develop a realistic timeline for executing all action steps

Task summary: Keeping momentum moving forward means that timelines must reflect reality. Those carrying out the action steps (i.e., the work!) need to agree to your timeline and be held accountable. Achieving buy-in to the timeline is one of your biggest challenges. Other things to think about to ensure that plans are implemented include establishing realistic time frames, identifying resources, and aligning plan objectives with annual operating plans and budgets.

Method: Answer the questions that follow (refer back to your work outline in Task 5; Timeline template available in the toolkit).

a) Is your timeline realistic? Do you have enough people involved to accomplish a specific task? Do you have the right people? Do you and they have enough time and money to accomplish the tasks? Who is the timekeeper?

b) Have you assigned leads to each task?

c) Have you identified the drivers for your timeline? Is there an accountability mechanism for these drivers? Do you have clear criteria for identifying success for each task?

d) Have you identified both existing and emerging barriers? What are your strategies for overcoming them?

e) Stakeholders: Is everyone in agreement? Is there broad consensus?

f) Stakeholders: How prescriptive or collaborative have you been about the time frame?

g) Have you identified what resources will be needed and how much those resources will cost?

h) Is your budget aligned with your strategic priorities?

i) Prioritizing objectives, strategies, and tasks helps in defining an appropriate timeline. How will you set your priorities for the strategies in your plan? Consider the following:

- Organizational readiness

- Staffing

- Budget

j) How will your plan get operationalized and integrated? How will it be woven into the fabric of the institution? How will you ensure that this plan will be recognized as a part of each person's job?

Timelines must reflect reality.

Tips

- A graphic of the various time frames should be created for reference.

- Timelines will keep you committed, focused, and accountable.

- You may need to be flexible with individual department needs.

- All resources below are available in the toolkit. Please see page 5 for link to toolkit.

Timeline Development Resource

- Office TIMELINE

Related Resources

- Assessing the Existing Landscape in Part II of the *Strategic Planning Guide*

- CFAR, Regional Health System Proposed Timeline and Process for Updating the Strategic Plan

Essential Task 9: Prepare the written plan

Task summary: As is obvious by now in the process, writing your strategic plan is a multifaceted job that will require coordination and various approvals. The details of the process should be reflected in your timeline.

Method: Review the sample strategic plans provided below.

Tips

- Do not feel constrained by templates or samples. The structure of your written plan should match your requirements.
- Review plans prepared by colleagues for inspiration.
- Implement your communication plan as you complete your written strategic plan.
- All resources below are available in the toolkit. Please see page 5 for link to toolkit.

Resources

Sample Strategic Plans:

- The George Washington University School of Medicine and Health Sciences Diversity and Inclusion Action Plan
- Rush University Medical Center Plan for Diversity and Inclusion
- Southern Illinois University School of Medicine Policy and Plan for Diversity and Inclusion
- University of Arizona College of Medicine–Phoenix Office Diversity and Inclusion Strategic Planning Map
- University of California, San Francisco, Strategic Plan for Diversity, Equity, and Inclusion
- The University of Kansas Medical Center Diversity and Inclusion Action Items
- University of Massachusetts Medical School Diversity Strategic Plan
- University of Texas Medical Branch Diversity Scorecard

Part II — Strategies to Meet Diversity and Inclusion Goals

Part I introduced nine essential tasks as a roadmap for the process of strategic planning. Part II expands on these essential tasks by offering specific strategies that could be included in a plan to meet diversity and inclusion goals, as well as tips for working with leadership and developing plan implementation skills as a diversity officer or institutional leader. Specifically, these sections cover why diversity is essential to an institution's strategic plan, who is responsible for creating and implementing the plan, what specific strategies could be included for achieving diversity and inclusion goals, and how to measure the effectiveness of a plan once implementation has begun.

The Case for Diversity and Inclusion

Related Tasks:

- Essential Task 1
- Essential Task 2

The first job for a diversity officer who is embarking on a strategic plan for diversity may be making the case for why diversity and inclusion should be included in strategic planning at all. This is especially important when gaining commitment from key stakeholders and assessing the current climate, as Tasks 1 and 2 show. This section begins with an overview of ways in which diversity proves vital to an academic medical center and ends with a case for excellence—the point of any strategic plan. Diversity does not occur along with excellence or in spite of it, but it is integral to the excellence and success of any institution.

The Accreditation Case

The Liaison Committee on Medical Education, the Accreditation Council for Graduate Medical Education, and the Joint Commission on Accreditation of Healthcare Organizations have established core regulatory and accreditation requirements for diversity and inclusion at academic health centers (AHCs).

The Liaison Committee on Medical Education (LCME) accredits medical education programs leading to the MD degree in the United States and Canada. Several LCME accreditation elements (formerly standards) relate to diversity in a medical school setting. These include diversity in the academic and learning environment, Element 3.3 (formerly IS-16 and MS-8), and cultural awareness in curricular content, Element 7.6 (formerly ED-21). To achieve and maintain accreditation, each medical education program must meet these LCME accreditation standards.

The text of these two key elements is as follows:

3.3 Diversity/Pipeline Programs and Partnerships
A medical school has effective policies and practices in place and engages in ongoing, systematic, and focused recruitment and retention activities, to achieve mission-appropriate diversity outcomes among its students, faculty, senior administrative staff, and other relevant members of its academic community.

These activities include the use of programs and/or partnerships aimed at achieving diversity among qualified applicants for medical school admission and the evaluation of program and partnership outcomes.[2]

7.6 Cultural Competence/Health Care Disparities/Personal Bias

The faculty of a medical school ensure that the medical curriculum provides opportunities for medical students to learn to recognize and appropriately address gender and cultural biases in themselves, in others, and in the health care delivery process. The medical curriculum includes instruction about:

- The manner in which people of diverse cultures and belief systems perceive health and illness and respond to various symptoms, diseases, and treatments
- The basic principles of culturally competent health care
- The recognition and development of solutions for health care disparities
- The importance of meeting the health care needs of medically underserved populations
- The development of core professional attributes (e.g., altruism, accountability) needed to provide effective care in a multidimensionally diverse society.[2]

For more information on these standards, visit the LCME website.

What is the cost of noncompliance with diversity and inclusion standards?

The Accreditation Council for Graduate Medical Education (ACGME) accredits postgraduate training of residents and fellows. ACGME program requirements state, "Residents *must* demonstrate interpersonal and communication skills that result in the effective exchange of information and collaboration with patients, their families, and health professionals."[3] ACGME standards also mandate the following:

Residents are expected to communicate effectively with patients, families, and the public, as appropriate, across a broad range of socioeconomic and cultural backgrounds (IV.A.5.d.1). Residents must demonstrate a commitment to carrying out professional responsibilities and adherence to ethical principles (IV.A.5.e.).[3]

Residents are expected to demonstrate compassion, integrity, and respect for others; responsiveness to patient needs that supersedes self-interest; respect for patient privacy and autonomy; accountability to patients, society, and the profession; and sensitivity and responsiveness to a diverse patient population, including, but not limited to, diversity in gender, age, culture, race, religion, disabilities, and sexual orientation (IV.A.5.e.1-5).[3]

The Joint Commission on Accreditation of Healthcare Organizations (JCAHO) has developed field guides for addressing effective communication, cultural competence, and patient- and family-centered care in hospitals and health care institutions.[4] These guides provide recommendations, self-assessments, strategies, practice examples, and resources to help hospitals address these issues. The most recent JCAHO field guide was developed to address the creation of a more welcoming, inclusive, and safe environment for the Lesbian, Gay, Bisexual, and Transgender (LGBT) community.[5]

What is the cost of noncompliance with diversity and inclusion standards? Failure to adequately address issues of AHC diversity and inclusion has resulted in punitive measures such as being placed on probation. Failure to advance diversity and inclusion severely affects an AHC's ability to eliminate health and health care disparities and move health equity forward.

In addition, an institutional climate that does not support diversity and inclusion as a core value to recruit and retain students, residents, faculty, and staff from a more diverse group limits the ability of diversity to serve as a driver of innovation and excellence.

The Legal Case

Institutional values and drivers vary throughout all academic institutions. An institution's culture often trumps all strategic plans and initiatives and is therefore important to assess and understand. Core values important to diversity and inclusion include social justice and the elimination of health disparities, but the legal drivers at some institutions may be at odds with them. Such legal drivers act as barriers and present additional challenges to recruiting and retaining a diverse and inclusive workforce. Eight states—California, Washington, Florida, Michigan, Nebraska, Arizona, New Hampshire, and Oklahoma—have laws that eliminate the use of race or ethnicity in admissions decisions.[6] Legislation in other states and pending federal cases may further impede progress and require additional engagement with legal counsel to ensure compliance with laws is maintained, but the mission to enhance diversity and inclusion can and must continue.

> Diversity should be a core value in the health professions. Health professions schools should ensure that their mission statements reflect a social contract with the community and a commitment to diversity among their students, faculty, staff, and administration.

The educational benefits of a diverse student body were affirmed by the U.S. Supreme Court in *Grutter v. Bollinger et al.* (2003), a case that involved the University of Michigan. The court's ruling held that "the educational benefits that flow from a diverse student body"may be a compelling interest for an institution of higher education. But the court left it to each university to determine whether such diversity is essential to its particular educational mission. According to the court's opinion, "Classroom discussion is livelier, more spirited, and simply more enlightened and interesting when students have the greatest possible variety of backgrounds."[7]

In *Fisher v. The University of Texas at Austin* (2013), the U.S. Supreme Court upheld *Grutter*. It did not, however, directly revisit the constitutionality of considering race as a factor in the college admissions process but instead vacated the circuit court's opinion in favor of the university and sent the case back to the 5th U.S. Circuit Court of Appeals. The Supreme Court ruled that the circuit court did not hold the university to the burden of proving it had applied a standard of strict scrutiny in accordance with *Grutter*.[8]

A 2004 report by the Sullivan Commission further delineated the benefits of diversity and the need for developing a critical mass of students of varying races and ethnic backgrounds. This report also emphasized the importance of unambiguous written institutional commitments to diversity. The commission declared, "Diversity should be a core value in the health professions. Health professions schools should ensure that their mission statements reflect a social contract with the community and a commitment to diversity among their students, faculty, staff, and administration."[9] Training a diverse health care workforce that is optimally prepared to care for a diverse population is a core mission and fundamental obligation of every medical school.

The Business Case

Patient satisfaction and patient outcomes have always been a primary concern for AHCs, but the Patient Protection and Affordable Care Act brings new urgency with the expansion of the pay-for-performance Medicare programs and an increased emphasis on the patient experience.[10]

One of the most important ways to provide quality care is to provide culturally competent care. Many times, poor outcomes are not the result of poor medical diagnoses but because of poor communication across language or cultural divides. The financial cost of patients returning to emergency departments with infections or for readmission is high. Frequently, readmissions occur because patients have inadequate knowledge of how to manage medications and how to follow clinical instructions. These costs are beginning to be transferred to the institution through changes in federal and state policies focused on quality and safety outcomes. Improved cultural competency and diversity in staff composition likely will benefit patient communication and therefore treatment outcomes and readmission rates.[11]

This is doubly important because of the startling health disparities that have not shifted in several decades. African-American, Hispanic, female, LGBT, and other minority groups experience worse health outcomes across a range of conditions, and closing the gap has become one of the most important mandates of AHCs in recent years.[12] Given that these minority groups will soon be in the majority in this country, these disparities are unacceptable.[13]

Given the vital role quality will play in the future of health care, the extremely diverse society in which we live, and the worrying disparities that exist, it is not only a moral obligation to diversify and invest in an inclusive climate at AHCs, but the only course that makes financial sense. No AHC can afford not to invest in diversity.

The Case for Excellence

There is persuasive evidence that recruiting a diverse student body and faculty has a strong, positive effect on the quality of medical education that is provided to learners. The positive educational outcomes include helping students break down stereotypes and racial biases; challenging assumptions; broadening perspectives about racial, ethnic, and cultural differences; and broadening students' understanding of the effects of language and culture on medical care—that is, achieving cultural competency.[14,15] The climate enhanced by a diverse learner and teacher body ultimately increases students' awareness of health and health care disparities in nearby populations and increases students' interest in service to underserved communities and overall civic commitment. These "added educational values" strengthen medical education and better prepare graduates to deliver health care services to an increasingly diverse population. More important, these educational benefits accrue for both minority and nonminority students.[16]

Assumptions are challenged, perspectives are broadened, and more socialization across a variety of racial and ethnic groups occurs, resulting in intellectual and cognitive benefits for all learners.

In a survey conducted at Harvard Medical School and the University of California, San Francisco, Medical School, students confirmed that concrete benefits accrue from a diverse student body. Students reported that contact with diverse peers led to a more balanced exchange of information in classroom discussions, more serious discussions of alternative viewpoints about disease and treatments, greater appreciation of inequities in the health care system, and more cultural sensitivity. According to the survey's authors, "Students regularly educate one another on important issues, such as differences among the cultures and how best to respond to those differences." Furthermore, students "established close collegial and personal friendships with students of different races and ethnicities, and such ties contributed greatly to their understanding of medical practice and, ultimately, better trained them for service in a multicultural society."[17]

A dividend of the diversity rationale is that diversity enhances the educational climate, and educational outcomes are directly improved as a result. Numerous studies have now demonstrated that for both medical students and residents, when diversity is integrated within the educational climate, assumptions are challenged, perspectives are broadened, and more socialization across a variety of racial and ethnic groups occurs, resulting in intellectual and cognitive benefits for all learners.[18–20] Greater diversity also helps ensure a more comprehensive and inclusive research agenda. These dividends can collectively drive academic institutions toward achieving excellence, which in turn will lead to improvement in health care equity through research and patient care for the populations served.

The Role of Diversity Officers

Related Tasks:

- Essential Task 4
- Essential Task 5
- Essential Task 6

The role of a diversity and inclusion leader is complex and challenging. It is not a one-size-fits-all position, and it has to be calibrated to match an institution's goals, history, culture, and priorities. Depending on the position within the organization, a diversity officer may be able to influence hundreds of people through a combination of diversity committees and councils, employee resource groups, dual reporting relationships, and accountability systems. This section includes the case for dedicated diversity officers, who are a necessary prerequisite for implementing any strategy for diversity, as well as resources for required leadership skills and tips for soliciting buy-in from senior leadership.

This section will be most useful in the completion of Tasks 4, 5, and 6 and will engage colleagues to create solutions that will truly move the needle toward diversity and inclusion. Creating a strategic plan is only the beginning; without the skills, the political capital, and the will to bring the plan to fruition, diversity planning is only an intellectual exercise.

The Case for Dedicated Diversity Officers

Diversity and inclusion officers and representatives at most AAMC-member schools have broad responsibilities that generally involve enhancing diversity and inclusion efforts in recruiting and supporting students underrepresented in medicine and biomedical sciences, trainees in graduate medical education programs, and faculty. Historically, some diversity officers may not have been directly involved in the process of diversifying the PhD-student population in the biomedical sciences. Given the imperative that exists in diversifying the biomedical research workforce, diversity officers have assisted in the recruitment of MD/PhD candidates. With the skill set that developed in this process, colleagues in charge of graduate school diversity programs can be successful. The skill set developed by diversity officers includes the following:

- Instituting holistic review
- Developing pipeline programs
- Creating and enhancing a nurturing climate for diversity
- Assisting the graduate school in its quest for student diversity

The case can be made that greater numbers of committed team members are required to advance the biomedical research workforce. Consider the following:

1. Compared with the general U.S. population, African-Americans, Hispanics, and Native Americans are severely underrepresented in the science, technology, engineering, and mathematics (STEM) fields and, consequently, in the biomedical research workforce.

2. In 2006, Hispanics and African-Americans accounted for 15 and 14 percent of the U.S. population, respectively. These groups earned only 5.2 and 4.5 percent, respectively, of doctoral degrees in STEM fields awarded to U.S. citizens by U.S. institutions in 2007.[21]

3. In 2010, Hispanics, African-Americans, and Native Americans together accounted for less than 30 percent of the U.S. population and in recent years have represented less than 9 percent of STEM PhD recipients.[22]

These data convey that despite the existence of diversity-focused research training programs, there is much work ahead to correct this problem of underrepresentation.

Many in the academic medicine community recognize that solutions to racial, ethnic, LGBT, and disability-related health disparities require a diverse physician and biomedical research workforce. This is best achieved through a team approach at each medical school, where diversity officers can collaborate with colleagues in graduate school administration. Innovative programs that emerge from the collective intellect of these parties may lead to ideas and programs uniquely suited for the culture of the medical schools.

Savvy diversity officers recognize the power dynamics embedded within the organizational structures of the institutions, departments, and programs they serve. A diversity officer who has no access to the executive office and is not a part of the leadership team will have a difficult time orchestrating meaningful change. Therefore, the positioning of the diversity officer role—within the organizational structure and in relation to the reporting hierarchy—is critical to success. It is ideal if the diversity officer reports directly to the dean (in the case of a medical school) or the chief executive officer (in an academic medical center). With the diversity officer so positioned, he or she should be given both the authority and joint accountability for key institutional outcomes. Although not an exhaustive list, some common areas a diversity officer can affect include student, faculty, and resident recruitment; institutional climate; and health disparities and health equity outcomes.

Savvy diversity officers recognize the power dynamics embedded within the organizational structures of the institutions, departments, and programs they serve.

Strategic Leadership

As this guide shows, strategy is critical to the role of a diversity officer. This section includes some of the ways diversity officers may be called upon to create and implement strategy: by acting as change agents, by being organizational consultants, or by standing aside to inspire others to take a leadership role in a diversity initiative. It also provides resources from other institutions' and medical schools' diversity efforts. True and lasting change occurs slowly at large institutions, and, often, timing is everything. Change can be best facilitated by aligning the diversity agenda with the values and goals of the leadership and the institution, while leveraging current internal and external pressures (e.g., accreditation standards) to drive forward motion.

The diversity leadership task is to plan and execute a strategy for the short and long term, focusing on achievable goals and easy "wins" along the way. Another aspect of strategy is identifying key stakeholders and allies who can be called upon for support, advice, and assistance. In fact, there will be times when it may not be advantageous for the diversity officer to take the lead in a diversity-related effort. In these situations, the diversity officer should ask, "Who is the best person to lead the charge with this particular issue and this particular audience?" Diversity work gains greater credibility and acceptance when thought leaders across the institution become visible allies and advocates.

A diversity officer also plays the role of an internal organizational consultant. This informal role can be a valuable way for the diversity officer to establish his or her value and demonstrate how diversity expertise can resolve real-world problems that arise in academic medicine. For example, a clerkship director might need guidance about accommodating the religious needs of a resident, or a program director believes that diversity training is needed because the demographics of the patient population have changed. In each case, there is an opportunity to educate and enlighten in a way that improves the organizational capacity to practice diversity and inclusion.

Resources

- Diversity Business Council, adapted from the Princeton University Diversity Council
- Cleveland Clinic Office of Diversity and Inclusion Toolkit, Annual Report, and Fact Sheet
- University of Massachusetts Medical School Diversity Toolkit
- University of California, San Francisco, Diversity Best Practices
- Auburn University School of Communication and Journalism Diversity Plan

The diversity leadership task is to plan and execute a strategy for the short and long term, focusing on achievable goals and easy "wins" along the way.

Developing Personal Leadership Skills

Organizations within academic medicine vary greatly; therefore, the function of the diversity officer can be very different from institution to institution.

The role of the diversity officer has become increasingly complex over the past several years for several key reasons. First, the scope of diversity and inclusion work in academic medicine has expanded greatly, often without commensurate resources. In addition, successful diversity and inclusion work means diversity officers must be change agents within a process of organizational transformation.[23] This means breaking new ground and at times advocating new concepts and methods that have not been considered previously. The territory can be uncharted, and scholarly literature has largely remained silent on the issue of how diversity affects leadership within the context of a multicultural society.[24]

Competencies a diversity officer needs

- Strategic vision
- Executive acumen
- Change management expertise and will
- Political savvy
- Persuasive communication
- Ability to navigate the culture of academic medicine
- Innovator's DNA
- Cultural intelligence
- Technical mastery of diversity and inclusion

Skill-strengthening tasks to complete

- Take an honest inventory of leadership strengths and weaknesses.
- Identify and seek out trusted colleagues—both internal and external—who provide objective feedback and perspectives.
- Take advantage of training, mentoring, and networking within professional organizations and other available resources.

Advice for new diversity officers

- Clarify the expectations, scope, and outcomes for the job. Follow with an analysis of the staffing needed to successfully meet the expected goals. These are crucial first steps.
- Negotiate for a program or project manager to help with the internal and external responsibilities.
- Understand what other resources are available to get the job done.
- Don't fall into the all-too-familiar trap of taking on all the diversity work.
- Create a communication strategy that educates key stakeholders about the role of the diversity office and how the office will work with them to accomplish the mission of the institution.
- Negotiate the way in which certain diversity-related tasks (e.g., data capture, programs, and diversity office inclusion in some processes) will be a shared responsibility.

> **Ultimately, diversity offices within academic medicine must be able to demonstrate the effectiveness of their efforts and initiatives.**

The diversity officer's job is both entrepreneurial and creative and will ideally include the support, freedom, and resources necessary to develop new initiatives for innovation around issues of diversity and inclusion. Resources are required to build new alliances, create partnerships, and influence behavior.

Ensuring that diversity and inclusion are included in the strategic plans of the institution is a key part of securing the resources and support a diversity officer needs to be effective in this role.

For more on these competencies, as well as other resources, see the AAMC guide The Role of the Chief Diversity Officer in Academic Health Centers.

Requisite Diversity Leadership Skills

Diversity work—by its very nature—requires that a diversity officer have or cultivate a unique set of leadership skills. At its foundation, the work mandates authenticity, a nonjudgmental perspective, a values-driven ethos, and the ability to signal to others a compassionate and understanding nature. Without these qualities, building the trust and credibility needed to move the work forward becomes difficult.

Strong interpersonal skills

- Ability to communicate with tact, diplomacy, and sophistication—diversity work involves having conversations about subject matter that is sensitive and at times uncomfortable. Often these crucial conversations involve pointing out a difficult or inconvenient truth or requesting that an individual change his or her behavior. Rather than a one-size-fits-all approach to communication, a diversity officer must anticipate the concerns and needs of diverse audiences and constituency groups.

- Ability to tailor communication to a particular audience—without compromising the integrity of the message

- Ability to build consensus—gather feedback, educate others, and respond to concerns so to advance the diversity work

Basic technical knowledge

- Solid understanding of the historical, legal, and sociocultural underpinnings of diversity, as well as an understanding of how these concepts apply to academic medicine

- Depth and breadth of knowledge of cultural competency, health equity, diverse workforce development, and organizational change concepts

- Knowledge on how decisions get made and who the informal and formal thought leaders in the organization are

Because the diversity office cannot do it all and should not become a silo, strong collaborative skills are necessary. Here are some tips to help support collaboration:

- Allot sufficient time to maintaining and developing relationships both internal and external to the institution.

- Create diversity councils to develop "ambassadors" for diversity work and to spread the influence of the diversity office beyond its narrow confines.

- Ensure membership of the diversity council reflects key departments and programs of the institution, and avoid being a "mutual diversity admiration society." In fact, a variety of viewpoints helps the diversity officer craft more realistic solutions to problems and often helps develop a greater depth of commitment among participants.

Senior Leadership Engagement

For any changes in the diversity of the institution to be successful and become fully integrated, it is essential that a full understanding of and support for diversity occur at multiple levels. That full buy-in and engagement occur throughout the entire institution is imperative, particularly among those in key leadership positions.

Each institution has its own culture; therefore, various approaches are needed to match the institutional culture. Specifically, the dean must achieve alignment with the senior leadership team, and the team, in turn, must align diversity both horizontally and vertically within the institution. This must occur within the culture of the institution as a whole and within the existing subcultures.

In addition to the dean, the governing board of an organization can be a powerful driver of diversity initiatives at an institution.

Below are questions that the board can pose to the dean or chief executive officer about the importance of diversity and inclusion at an institution.

- **Strategic Plan**
  - o What efforts have been made to integrate issues of diversity and inclusion into the day-to-day academic and clinical lives of the institution's faculty, learners, and staff?
- **Resources**
  - o What resources (e.g., finance or personnel) are committed to and focused on the objective of increasing diversity and inclusion?
  - o What has been the return on investment of these resources? Are additional resources needed to meet the objectives?
- **Performance Measures/Evaluations**
  - o Is the executive leadership of the organization evaluated on the promotion of diversity initiatives as part of the performance evaluation process?
- **Human Capital**
  - o What types of support have been made available to diversity leaders? These support mechanisms can include (1) support staff, (2) funding, (3) opportunities for continued education (about diversity and medical education, bias, crucial conversations, building cultural competence, legal implications surrounding diversity issues), (4) inclusion in leadership committees (with other deans, section heads, department chiefs, etc.), and (5) voice in building (or regularly reviewing) mission statements, climate surveys, data collection and analysis.
  - o Are diversity-promoting activities taken into account for faculty promotion, and if not, why not?

- **Organizational Capacity**
  - o How do you know that inclusion truly exists and the voices around the table are diverse and being heard? Please provide examples.

Resources

- *Academic Medicine* journal articles on diversity and inclusion
- The AAMC Group on Diversity and Inclusion Member Resources, including databases and education

Assessing the Existing Landscape

Related Tasks:

- Essential Task 2

Assessing the Current Climate and Culture of Diversity and Inclusion

When undertaking any change initiative, the current climate is as important as any future goal. Imagine trying to use a GPS that can only find a destination, not a current location; it would be useless. There are a number of ways to carry out an assessment, but the most useful is a mix of qualitative and quantitative data gathering. Begin with the Data Collection Self-Assessment in Task 2 for more information on assessing the current climate.

Good sources of qualitative data are reflective exercises, interviews, and focus groups. There are many resources available to frame these discussions, but whatever reflection is undertaken (e.g., interviews held with stakeholders or focus groups representing key samples of the population), the best way to take the pulse of any organization is to solicit information. Focus groups could consist of diverse and homogenous groups; both types may provide rich data. For instance, a focus group could consist of only faculty or students, or it could be divided instead by ethnic group, sexual orientation, or another category. Alternatively, focus groups could consist of a mix of identities and roles.

One of the most important things diversity officers can do is engage in self-reflection about the culture, climate, and diversity of their institutions. Strategic planning is the perfect time to take a step back from the day-to-day details and examine goals. It is a time to consider the wider community and the history, policies, practices, and procedures affecting diversity, and it is a time to consider the current makeup and climate of the institution.

Regarding quantitative information, conducting a survey of key interest groups or soliciting an outside consultant to complete an evaluation would be valuable. Historical data are also available from the AAMC and offer demographic information and student survey satisfaction data specific to institutions, in addition to national averages.

If a diversity officer does not have expertise in evaluating data, she or he will need to work with someone who does. Finding those experts at an institution and soliciting help or hiring appropriate outside consultants are necessary to accomplishing this step.

Resources

- AAMC Diversity Engagement Survey
- Assessing Institutional Climate and Culture Webcast
- AAMC Data and Analysis
- AAMC Diversity Facts and Figures Data Series

Evaluating the Success of Strategic Plans

Ultimately, diversity offices within academic medicine must be able to demonstrate the effectiveness of their efforts and initiatives. An analysis of the data necessary to address accreditation, funding, and program evaluation needs is a good place to start. It is not unusual to find that multiple data sources will need to be tapped to develop a comprehensive diversity outcomes "dashboard." Once established, however, diversity outcome data serve many vital purposes.

Tracking year-to-year changes in diversity measures can reflect progress made and reveal work that still needs to be done, thereby influencing resources and decisions. The dissemination of an annual diversity report that summarizes successes in the areas of recruitment, retention, cultural competency, and institutional climate builds credibility for the diversity office and educates others about the scope and significance of the work.

After the first year of strategic planning, it is important to evaluate established strategic plans continuously to determine whether objectives have been achieved. For quantitative data especially, the exact same metric must be used each time to be able to compare data over time. The best argument for further support and funding of diversity initiatives is proof that previous endeavors have been successful and have contributed to the organization's overall strategic goals.

Here are other ways to evaluate diversity strategic planning initiatives:

1. **Community Feedback.** Solicit feedback from people in the surrounding community to gauge the success of efforts in community engagement.
2. **Training and Education Evaluations.** Collect employee evaluations of diversity training, and record diversity training completion rates.
3. **Attitude Surveys.** Conduct surveys to determine how students, faculty, and staff feel about the implementation of the diversity initiatives.
4. **Exit Interviews and Surveys.** Leverage the exit surveys of graduating students (including those who leave the institution before graduation) and departing faculty and staff to gauge perceptions of the diversity initiatives.
5. **Philanthropic Involvement.** Track the number of hours spent volunteering with diversity-related groups or for diversity-related causes.
6. **Affinity Network Activities.** Measure the activities of affinity groups, with records of attendance and how often events took place.
7. **Diversity Spending.** Track the amount of money spent on maintaining events held by the affinity networks or other diversity-related gatherings.
8. **Leadership Communication.** Track organizational and/or executive appearances in diversity-related media, such as internal and external speeches.

> **After the first year of strategic planning, it is important to evaluate established strategic plans continuously to determine whether objectives have been achieved.**

Achieving Diversity and Inclusion

Related Tasks:

- Essential Task 4

In a sense, strategy is nothing more than an exercise in making choices. There are endless opportunities and problems with an infinite number of solutions, but no single individual or institution has unlimited resources, bandwidth, or time to deal with them all. The strategic planning process is a way to identify where efforts and resources are going to have the most impact and also a way to consciously choose from which initiatives to disengage.

When choosing an initiative, there is an automatic cost incurred by all of the projects moving forward. Depending on the initiatives, this cost may be that high school students do not get to participate in a premedical education night, medical students do not get help selecting the right residency, or minority faculty do not get assurances when trying to make the decision to work at an institution.

The completion of Assessing the Existing Landscape in Task 2 and Identify Leverage Points and Challenges in Task 3 should reveal where to begin diversity and inclusion strategic planning so that it will have the greatest impact for your institution. Perhaps the first goal should be addressing areas of greatest need—for example, LCME accreditation or the dismal climate for MD/PhD students of color. Perhaps it should be a small step or an easy win. Senior leadership may already be invested in increasing recruitment for faculty of color, or the institution may already have a good relationship with local community partners; such small goals have an important place in a strategic plan as well.

For many more decisions, however, there will be many strategic priorities from which to choose, and diversity officers need to be selective in the interventions they can reasonably expect to implement. The following sections on achieving diversity at every level of an institution are designed to help in this process. Each subsection includes additional ideas for creating interventions in areas such as financial aid and faculty recruitment.

This section can be used in one of two ways: for inspiration on what to address in a current strategic plan (and therefore what not to address) or as a reference if specific issues (e.g., faculty retention, K–12 partnerships) have already been prioritized.

> **Diversity officers need to be selective in the interventions they can reasonably expect to implement.**

Achieving Inclusion

Without an inclusive culture, a diversity strategy may be in danger of becoming a taskforce to count people. Research indicates that inclusive environments boost the capacity of medical schools to excel and ensure health equity for all.

Diversity 3.0 Framework

In 2012, the AAMC convened a group of experts to discuss essential elements of institutional culture and climate around diversity and inclusion and to begin considering ways of comprehensively assessing culture and climate to increase an institution's capacity to build more diverse and inclusive environments. Based on extensive literature reviews and feedback from experts in the field, the AAMC developed the Diversity 3.0 Framework to support innovative, high-performing organizations in promoting a culture of inclusion and a full appreciation of different perspectives. Whereas Diversity 1.0 and 2.0 were peripheral efforts that emphasized solving the problems of inadequate representation and barriers, Diversity 3.0 integrates activities and policies into core organizational strategies. It views diversity and inclusion as solutions instead of problems.

CULTURE OF DIVERSITY & INCLUSION IN ACADEMIC MEDICINE
Diversity 3.0 Framework

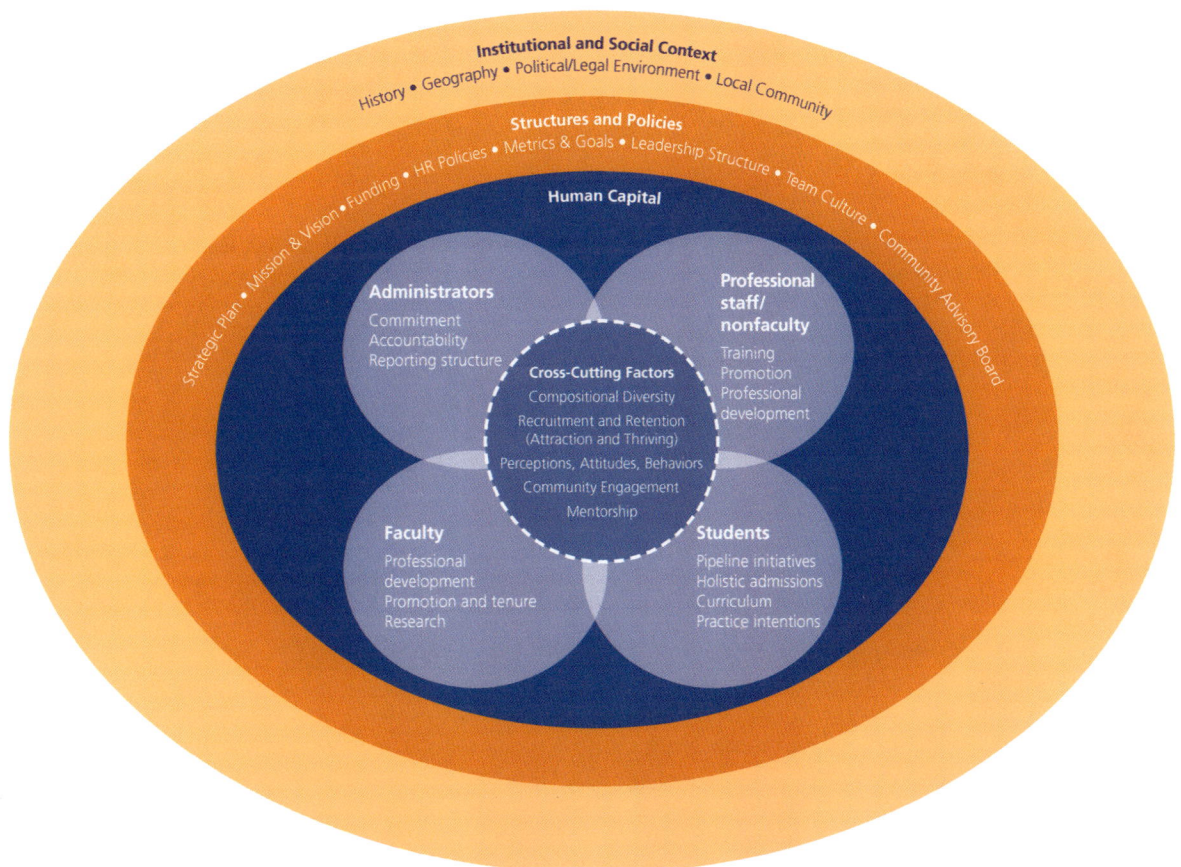

Institutional and Social Context
History • Geography • Political/Legal Environment • Local Community

Structures and Policies
Strategic Plan • Mission & Vision • Funding • HR Policies • Metrics & Goals • Leadership Structure • Team Culture • Community Advisory Board

Human Capital

Administrators
Commitment
Accountability
Reporting structure

Professional staff/nonfaculty
Training
Promotion
Professional development

Cross-Cutting Factors
Compositional Diversity
Recruitment and Retention (Attraction and Thriving)
Perceptions, Attitudes, Behaviors
Community Engagement
Mentorship

Faculty
Professional development
Promotion and tenure
Research

Students
Pipeline initiatives
Holistic admissions
Curriculum
Practice intentions

The previous Diversity 3.0 Framework highlights three key dimensions of diversity and inclusion:

- **Institutional and Social Context.** The external forces affecting people and processes within institutions that shape expectations and experiences. Factors that influence culture such as history, geography, political and legal environments, and local community fall in this dimension.

- **Structures and Policies.** The processes, practices, and procedures within institutions that act as barriers or accelerators of culture. Such factors include the institution's strategic plan, mission and vision, funding, human resource policies, metrics and goals, leadership structure, team culture, and the community advisory board.

- **Human Capital.** The people—administrators, faculty, professional staff/nonfaculty, and students—make the place. Compositional diversity, recruitment and retention, perceptions, attitudes, behaviors, community engagement, and mentorship determine culture. There are particular issues facing each of these groups that are important components of culture. For example, professional development programs for faculty represent an important facet of culture.

For more information, please watch the Assessing Institutional Climate & Culture webcast

Diversity Works, Inc., a company that offers diversity education, also provides a framework for creating an inclusive climate, which identifies five key factors:

- **Education and Scholarship.** This factor includes actions such as valuing and hiring expertise in community-engaged scholarship, cultural competence, and health disparities and approaching diversity as an added value and not a cost.

- **Community Connections.** This factor concerns the wider community. Key things to consider are perceptions of an "ivory tower" in the community's midst and interactions between the university community and the local community.

- **Climate and Culture.** This factor involves how welcomed and supported people feel, as well as quantitative measures of diversity and whether any individual is the lone representative of a group.

- **Representation and Voice.** This factor concerns the status quo and how routinely those in power listen to and address diverse concerns.

- **Institutional Transformation.** This factor involves the nature of institutional policies and procedures. Institutional policies should eliminate discrimination or outdated rhetoric and move toward policies that are more inclusive.

Resources

- AAMC Diversity Engagement Survey
- Assessing Institutional Climate and Culture Webcast
- AAMC Diversity 3.0 Learning Series

Throughout the remainder of this section are more resources for developing inclusion and about diversity for students, faculty, and administrators.

Achieving Student Diversity

Only by harnessing the entire diverse human capital of an academic medical center can the institution's mission be achieved. The work of recruiting, retaining, and advancing individuals from underrepresented groups in medicine and biomedical sciences—whether students, faculty, or residents—relies on a diverse team of talent managers. The work of cultural competence education is supported by diversity of thought and perspectives across all disciplines and all levels in the institution. The work of reducing health care disparities extends to all health care providers, researchers, and support staff. Thus, it is imperative that any diversity strategic plan gives attention to the recruitment, retention, and advancement of diversity and inclusion across the continuum of training and employment.

Medical student diversity is a key centerpiece for any institution's approach to strategic planning for diversity and inclusion. It is essential that an institution's strategic plan address the many facets of this important part of the educational experience. The Group on Student Affairs (GSA), the GSA Committee on Student Diversity Affairs (COSDA), and the GSA-COSDA representatives play a key role in the activities and programs that focus on the K–12, premedical, and medical education components of the educational spectrum. The following sections address issues and activities that an institution should incorporate into its strategic planning approach, including K–12 partnerships and pipeline programs, premedical students, medical student recruitment and selection, medical student retention and career development, introduction to graduate medical education, and financial counseling and support.

Only by harnessing the entire diverse human capital of an academic medical center can the institution's mission be achieved.

Premedical School

K–12 Partnerships and Pipeline Programs

The LCME requires investment in pipeline programs with Element 3.3 (formerly IS-16 and MS-8). Components include exposure to health professions, community investment/outreach, applicant preparation/applicant pool enhancement, and direct recruitment and matriculation. The context of pipeline programs is broad. Many schools have supported pipeline programs for decades; others are just beginning or expanding programming. The recent federal-funding cuts to Title VII have had vast negative impacts on pipeline programs at schools nationwide. It is now considered best practice for institutions to fully fund programs deemed essential to the school's mission, while securing grant support to supplement or temporarily expand the service reach. Any pipeline program established through grant funding should have an associated long-term funding commitment from the institution.

Partnerships and programs serving the K–12 constituency contribute an important part of the educational outreach continuum. K–12 partnerships may include adopting a school and providing assistance with reading programs, health literacy, and improvements to math and science instruction. There also may be programs developed by the medical school that target specific grade levels and populations. Programs are usually most successful when incorporating hands-on lessons and experiential learning. Hands-on experiences include dissection, suturing, gram staining, and DNA extraction. Experiential learning often involves a mini medical school approach that covers problem-based learning, research lab visits, basic physical exam skills, and mentorship from current medical students.

Clarifying the purpose of the K–12 partnership or the K–12 program is key to assessing outcomes and results. Positive "brand" recognition from the community is measured differently than applicant pool enhancement. Evaluation metrics for outreach programs are important for accreditation purposes and program improvement, and they may provide scholarly research opportunities for faculty and students. Assessment tools may include pre- and post-surveys, focus groups from community members or program participants, school-based metrics (such as reading levels or competencies), or enrollment/performance measures. Both research-related endeavors and service endeavors contribute to LCME element (formerly standards) fulfillment (Element 3.2, formerly IS-14).

Resources

- Community-Campus Partnerships for Health
- University Neighborhood Partners
- Health Resources and Services Administration Health Careers Opportunities Program (HCOP)
- Health Resources and Services Administration Centers of Excellence (COE)
- Stanford Mini Med School
- U.S. Department of Health and Human Services, Health Resources and Services Administration, Bureau of Health Professions, Office of Public Health and Science, Office of Minority Health. 2009. Pipeline Programs to Improve Racial and Ethnic Diversity in the Health Professions: An Inventory of Federal Programs, Assessment of Evaluation Approaches, and Critical Review of the Research Literature.
- DeLisa JA, Thomas P. 2005. Physicians with disabilities and the physician workforce: a need to reassess our policies. American Journal of Physical Medicine & Rehabilitation 84(5):11.

Premedical Students

Institutions should provide quality resources and a strong network of support for all premedical students. Of particular importance is consistent and reliable advising support, which can be difficult to procure for underrepresented, first-generation, LGBT, nontraditional, disabled, and low-income students. Often, these students are "homeless" when it comes to gaining access to helpful information about their specific situation. They may experience financial challenges in completing coursework, or they may not know how to apply to medical school if unable to access support from their undergraduate institution. Advising structures in undergraduate institutions may not meet the needs of all students or may provide inaccurate and discouraging information.

Providing premedical advising support to students underrepresented in medicine should be incorporated into the medical school strategic plan. These services may be accessed through any designated office provided that specific efforts are made to incorporate a proactive and comprehensive approach. An office that advises only students at the doorstep is most likely not meeting the needs of those underrepresented in medicine. Strategies to implement support may include development of outreach/enrichment programs that enhance the preparation of premedical students; participation in recruitment fairs, student conferences, and college information programs; creation of targeted advertisements; and establishment of formal relationships with advisors and professors from undergraduate institutions. It is also important to connect with organizations such as the National Association of Advisors for the Health Professions (NAAHP) and use the materials and resources offered by the AAMC. Policies and selection criteria should be fully transparent to prospective students, especially policies of the American Medical College Application Service® (AMCAS®). (Refer to LCME Elements 10. 3, 10.4, and 3.3, formerly MS-3, MS-5, and MS-8.)

Resources

- National Association of Advisors for the Health Professions
- National Association for College Admission Counseling
- AAMC Resources for Pre-Health Advisors
- American Educational Research Association
- Educators for Fair Consideration
- Liaison Committee on Medical Education

Postbaccalaureate Students

A special aspect of premedical advising involves working with students who have completed a baccalaureate degree and are not yet ready to enter medical school. This group of students includes a highly diverse set of learners: those who were premedical students but did not perform strongly in undergraduate studies, individuals who are seeking to strengthen their background in the sciences before applying to medical school, and individuals who have been unsuccessful in gaining entry to medical school. Regardless of whether the institution has a formal program for postbaccalaureate students, it is important that advising be offered to these students. This advising could include referral to a program offered by the institution, referral to a formal postbaccalaureate program at another institution, or advice on the classes that should be taken as a part of student-organized postbaccalaureate coursework.

Resources

- AAMC Postbaccalaureate Premedical Programs

Medical Student Recruitment and Selection

Recruiting a diverse class of trainees is essential at all levels. Recruitment involves working with the applicant pool, interview decisions, offers, and matriculation. Across all of these phases, collaboration, information sharing, and outcomes analysis are essential to success.

Applicant Pool Phase

A medical school must recognize that recruitment strategies begin in pipeline opportunities, as noted in the previous section. Schools should consider investing time and/or resources in undergraduate institutions and other groups involved with premedical preparation and advising. Schools should be aware that the AAMC has information on the applicant pool that will be useful in crafting a recruitment strategy with achievable goals relative to a school's mission and enrollment targets. Many medical student organizations that serve groups underrepresented in medicine—Student National Medical Association (SNMA), Latino Medical Student Association (LMSA), Association of Native American Medical Students (ANAMS)—have premedical groups. Recruiters and individuals working with prospective applicants should have access to admissions information, and schools should work to ensure that any access complies with Family Educational Rights and Privacy Act (FERPA) standards. Schools also should work with premedical advisors to ensure they are informed about qualifications of the ideal candidate. LGBT students present unique challenges for recruitment because they are currently unable to categorically self-identify on the AMCAS® application. Schools might therefore consider including positive LGBT messages in recruitment materials.

Interview Phase

Once applicants are invited for interviews, schools should have in place a process incorporating diversity. This might include the following options:

- Scheduling a critical mass of underrepresented minority students on the same day

- Engaging the campus diversity and inclusion office

- Including an information session about diversity during the interview day for all candidates

- Providing a printed information summary of programming and resources related to diversity for all candidates

- Providing outreach mechanisms during the interview day by partnering with the diversity and inclusion office to connect prospective LGBT students with current ones

Matriculation Phase

The process for matriculation of students will be specific to each institution. This phase begins after a student has received an acceptance. Schools should recognize that students who receive multiple offers may need additional information and support to make a final decision and should be prepared to provide information on scholarship and grant availability, school climate, school curriculum and cocurriculum, overall cost, and additional factors. A second-look visit is a common strategy used by schools to provide additional information and incentives for matriculation. However, second-look programs cannot be mandatory and should be designed so as not to disenfranchise students with limited financial means. Schools can provide information related to diverse students as part of such a program. Reaching out to accepted students through personal phone calls can also be very effective.

Resources

- AspiringDocs
- Summer Medical and Dental Education Program (SMDEP)
- Minority Student Medical Career Awareness Workshops and Recruitment Fair
- Medical Minority Applicant Registry (Med-MAR)
- Medical School Admission Requirements® (MSAR®)
- Association of American Medical Colleges (AAMC)

Medical School

Medical Student Retention and Career Development

A successful strategic plan will incorporate a significant component that addresses how services will be delivered to students from diverse backgrounds once they matriculate into medical school. The graduation of these students is the ultimate measure of success for a medical school's diversity and inclusion strategic plan. Therefore, it is critical that each medical school identify the structure and delivery of resources and services. At many institutions, there is a designated diversity and inclusion office that organizes and provides crucial academic and social support services. A strategic plan's structure and model can vary from institution to institution, but that plan must include the services to be delivered to support the enrolled medical students.

> **The ultimate measure of success for a medical school's diversity and inclusion strategic plan for medical students is the graduation of those students.**

Academic Support Structures

Diverse students arrive at medical school with a wide spectrum of experiences and skills, making academic support structures vital. Student affairs and/or diversity and inclusion offices, working collaboratively with course directors, academic support offices (medical school or main campus), wellness offices, and others, need to offer services that will identify student challenges and improve performance. Some students experiencing academic difficulty will not seek help independently; therefore, identifying students in need and intervening early are crucial. Multiple support systems that use varied approaches with structured, consistent intervention and monitoring best serve adult learners, particularly those from diverse backgrounds who enter medical school. There are many options for educational support:

- Prematriculation programs
- Monitoring and intervention by front-line faculty, unit directors, student affairs office, or diversity and inclusion office
- Tutorial programs
- Academic support offices (to assist with block/course/clerkship-specific learning and test-taking skills, individualized study plans/schedules, identifying and using resources specific to medical school, USMLE Step I and Step II preparation, remediation, etc.)
- Academic/learning/cognitive assessment
- General enhancement (e.g., assistance with reading speed and comprehension, learning strategies that are not content specific, test-taking strategies, time management, and group-study skills)
- Disability resources and accommodations
- Wellness assessment and programs

Social Support Services

The office of diversity and inclusion and the office of student affairs often play a critical role in students' adjustment to the medical school environment. For students to survive and thrive, the institutional climate must be welcoming and supportive. Mentoring and encouraging participation in student/professional organizations are two key strategies that an institution can offer to help students build professional connections. The types of mentoring include faculty to student, resident to student, student to student, community physician to student, and group. Each type of mentoring provides different levels of support. Creating a mentoring or advising structure that is a formal part of the student support offered should be incorporated into the strategic plan. An office of diversity and inclusion is one such place where these crucial social support structures can be fostered.

Once enrolled in medical school, students often wish to organize and give back to their communities; therefore, medical schools need to be supportive of student groups that promote inclusion. Several of these organizations are listed in the resources section below. Involvement in student and professional organizations is one way that students underrepresented in medicine can develop a sense of purpose for their professional growth. An institution's financial support of student involvement and financial support for student leaders to attend national conferences also are important.

> **The office of diversity and inclusion and office of student affairs often play a critical role in students' adjustment to the medical school environment.**

Resources

- Asian Pacific American Medical Student Association
- Association of American Indian Physicians
- Association of Native American Medical Students
- Gay and Lesbian Medical Association
- Latino Medical Student Association
- Medical Students with Disabilities Resource Guide
- National Hispanic Medical Association
- National Medical Association
- Student National Medical Association

Financial Counseling and Support

With the rising costs of an education that is already expensive, understanding the importance of financial aid for students pursuing a career as a health professional is essential. The office of financial aid and/or financial aid officers must be strategically included in the pipeline programs, student recruitment, and student retention agendas coordinated by the offices of admissions, student affairs, diversity and inclusion, and outreach. The role of the director/dean of financial aid is to keep deans and administrators of these offices abreast of federal and institutional financial aid matters because it provides a consistent across-the-board message to students. Successful agendas must have purposeful and strategic ongoing communication with trained financial aid administrators and personnel to address the emotional and social challenges associated with poverty. A successful strategic plan should also encourage staff from the development office and alumni relations to work closely with the offices of admissions, diversity and inclusion, and financial aid.

Resources

- Federal Student Aid (U.S. Department of Education)
- AAMC Financial Aid Officer Handbook
- AAMC Financial Information, Resources, Services, and Tools (FIRST)
- AAMC Loan Repayment/Forgiveness and Scholarship Programs searchable database
- AAMC Organization of Student Representatives (OSR) Resources
- Herbert W. Nickens Medical Student Scholarships for underrepresented students in medicine

Career Development and Residency Preparation

The ultimate goal of a medical student is to practice in his/her chosen specialty of medicine. The office of student affairs often delivers career counseling and development services. Care must be given to ensure that advising students who are underrepresented in medicine provides them with exposure to the broad range of options available and not a predetermined subset. A strategic plan should incorporate a process designed to meet the specific needs of students who may not know physicians who come from diverse backgrounds themselves or who work with diverse patients. Varied experiences, service learning opportunities, and contacts with community-based organizations are critical. The AAMC, through its Careers in Medicine® (CiM) program, offers significant resources to help students understand how their interests and skills apply to certain career options.

Resources

- AAMC Careers in Medicine
- AAMC Choices Newsletter

Achieving Resident Diversity

Residency Recruitment

The final component of the medical student educational continuum connects to the beginning of the graduate medical education process. The most effective process for diversifying residency programs is conducted in the context of an institution-wide commitment to diversity. In addition to leadership, significant factors for success include active recruitment of residency applicants outside standard networks, thoughtful composition and training of residency selection committees (including training on unconscious bias), defined metrics for candidate assessment, and a supportive and inclusive campus climate. The Accreditation Council for Graduate Medical Education (ACGME) accredits postgraduate training of residents and fellows. ACGME standards state that residents must demonstrate competencies that include professionalism—the major components of which include commitment, adherence, and sensitivity.[25]

> **The most effective process for diversifying residency programs is conducted in the context of an institution-wide commitment to diversity.**

The institutional strategic plan should address the recruitment of students into residency programs. Recruitment practices should include defining expectations for diversity of the residency program applicant pool and interviewees based on AAMC data; development of an annual programmatic evaluation that includes elements such as number of underrepresented residents relative to availability pool and satisfaction by race/ethnicity;[26] development of institutional partnerships and collaborations to improve the applicant pool and connections with service communities; and development of specific recruitment strategies. A small sample of promising practices is provided below.

Recruitment Strategies Promising Practices

- Visiting Medical Student Clerkships. Establish a visiting scholars program and encourage diverse medical students to spend four to six weeks in a visiting clinical clerkship on your campus. This program facilitates the visibility of students within the subsequent residency selection process.

- "Diversity Days" for Interviews across Programs. On designated days within the interview cycle, applicants are provided an opportunity to meet diverse residents and faculty from various academic departments.

- Second-Look Visits. Host an opportunity for applicants to return to the campus for a second look at the program and to learn more about the support, culture, and climate of the institution.

- Initiatives for Women. Although women outnumber men in primary care, gender parity lags behind in many specialties, including orthopedics, ophthalmology, urology, radiology, and certain surgical specialties. Both online and in person, highlight the experience of senior female physicians, especially in these specialties. Host meet-and-greets where aspiring female medical students can speak to these mentors candidly about work-life balance and the climate of the hospital.

Residency Training

The ACGME is responsible for the accreditation of post-MD medical training programs within the United States. It dictates six core competencies residents must achieve. Culturally competent care and effective treatment of diverse patients are woven into these competencies and are explicitly stated in Number 5. The six core competencies are as follows:

1. Patient Care. Residents must provide care that is compassionate, appropriate, and effective for the treatment of health problems and the promotion of health.

2. Medical Knowledge. Residents must have knowledge about established and evolving biomedical, clinical, and cognate (e.g., epidemiological and social-behavioral) sciences and apply this knowledge to patient care.

3. Practice-Based Learning and Improvement. Residents must be able to investigate and evaluate their care of patients care, appraise and assimilate of scientific evidence, and improve patient care.

4. Interpersonal and Communication Skills. Residents must demonstrate an effective information exchange and collaboration with patients, their families, and other health professionals.

5. Professionalism. Residents must commit to carrying out professional responsibilities, adherence to ethical principles, and sensitivity to a diverse patient population.

6. Systems-Based Practice. Residents must demonstrate an awareness of and responsiveness to the larger context and system of health care and the ability to effectively call on system resources to provide care that is of optimal value.[27]

Strategies for Addressing the Professionalism Requirement

1. Compassion, integrity, and respect for others

2. Responsiveness to patients needs that supersedes self-interest

3. Respect for patient privacy and autonomy

4. Accountability to patients, society, and the profession

5. Sensitivity and responsiveness to a diverse patient population, including, but not limited to, diversity in gender, age, culture, race, religion, disabilities, and sexual orientation

Professionalism supports a climate of respect and equity in which diversity can thrive. It is imperative that medical school faculty also demonstrate and reinforce the importance of the professionalism standard.

Residents play a critical role not only in the care of patients, but also in the clinical education of medical students. Furthermore, a diverse and engaged body of residents is an internal pipeline for faculty positions. Below is a list of potential barriers and possible approaches to achieving resident diversity.

> **Residents play a critical role not only in the care of patients, but also in the clinical education of medical students.**

Potential Barriers

- Metrics. Residency programs often evaluate candidates based on a small set of metrics (focused mostly on test scores), which may not be the best metrics to find the class of future doctors they aspire to train. To combat this, residence program directors and department chairs can identify the metrics by which leaders are evaluated for accountability to diversity.

    o Individual performance appraisals. Define expectations for diversity of the applicant pool and interviewees based on AAMC data.

    o An annual programmatic evaluation. Conduct an evaluation that uses a report card methodology, noting, for example, the number of underrepresented in medicine applicants relative to the availability pool and satisfaction by race/ethnicity.[26]

- Potential for isolation within a given subspecialty. Residency programs must establish institutional partnerships and collaborations to facilitate the development of communities. This is of particular importance when residents may lack race/ethnicity, LGBT, or disability-concordant peers or role models within their own division or department. By leveraging diversity across the institution, the feeling of inclusion and belonging can be enhanced.

- Differential rates of matching internal medical students to residency programs. Institutions should evaluate the match rate for underrepresented minorities from their medical schools to their residencies in comparison with the match rate for non-Hispanic white students.

Approaches

- Leadership

    o Mission, vision, and values. These must be inclusive of diversity, articulated by the dean, and reflected in administration, key committee appointments, websites, and invited speakers.

    o Accountability. Campus-wide evidence of the importance of diversity is essential, as are clearly defined metrics for measuring success.

- Welcoming/Inclusive Climate

    o Social Support. Facilitate interactions across residency programs to prevent isolation and enhance the development of community.

    o Role Models. Seek physicians from the community to engage with residents when there are inadequate numbers within your faculty ranks.

    o Mentors. Establish a mentoring program for residents, with training for mentors so they recognize and are sensitive to mentoring across differences. Also provide opportunities for residents to serve as mentors for medical students.

Achieving Graduate (PhD) Diversity

Graduate Diversity Strategies

In 2010, when Latinos/Hispanics, African-Americans, and American Indians accounted for more than 30 percent of the U.S. population, less than 9 percent of individuals from those groups obtained PhDs in science, technology, engineering, and mathematics (STEM) fields.[28,29] However, this rather bleak statistic is in many ways misleading for biomedical graduate student education. Within the STEM fields, physics, mathematics, and engineering traditionally have been slow to accommodate minorities and women. However, the biomedical sciences field is an exception, and many within it have worked for decades to improve minority representation.

In 1980, approximately 2 percent of underrepresented minorities enrolled in graduate programs in the biomedical sciences (i.e., biology, biochemistry, and chemistry). Compare this with 2010 when there was an increase to 11 percent.[30]

Graduate programs in the biomedical sciences (and STEM fields in general) would increase the number of students from underrepresented groups who earn PhDs if the pipeline of individuals obtaining bachelor's degrees in the biomedical sciences (and other STEM fields) was strengthened. This causal relationship speaks to a broader issue of underrepresentation throughout the educational spectrum. The figure below illustrates a framework for strengthening the pipeline and enhancing an institution's ability to create and sustain a diversified graduate program.

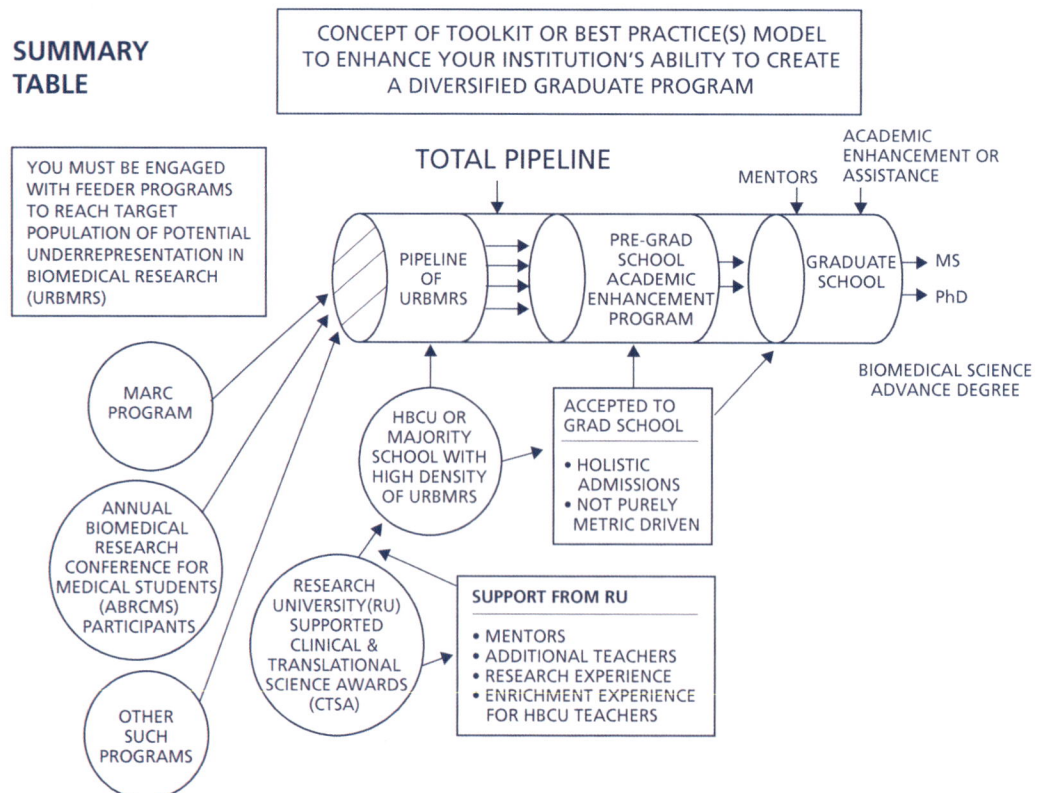

SUMMARY TABLE

CONCEPT OF TOOLKIT OR BEST PRACTICE(S) MODEL TO ENHANCE YOUR INSTITUTION'S ABILITY TO CREATE A DIVERSIFIED GRADUATE PROGRAM

YOU MUST BE ENGAGED WITH FEEDER PROGRAMS TO REACH TARGET POPULATION OF POTENTIAL UNDERREPRESENTATION IN BIOMEDICAL RESEARCH (URBMRS)

TOTAL PIPELINE

MENTORS

ACADEMIC ENHANCEMENT OR ASSISTANCE

PIPELINE OF URBMRS

PRE-GRAD SCHOOL ACADEMIC ENHANCEMENT PROGRAM

GRADUATE SCHOOL → MS → PhD

BIOMEDICAL SCIENCE ADVANCE DEGREE

MARC PROGRAM

ANNUAL BIOMEDICAL RESEARCH CONFERENCE FOR MEDICAL STUDENTS (ABRCMS) PARTICIPANTS

OTHER SUCH PROGRAMS

HBCU OR MAJORITY SCHOOL WITH HIGH DENSITY OF URBMRS

RESEARCH UNIVERSITY(RU) SUPPORTED CLINICAL & TRANSLATIONAL SCIENCE AWARDS (CTSA)

ACCEPTED TO GRAD SCHOOL

- HOLISTIC ADMISSIONS
- NOT PURELY METRIC DRIVEN

SUPPORT FROM RU

- MENTORS
- ADDITIONAL TEACHERS
- RESEARCH EXPERIENCE
- ENRICHMENT EXPERIENCE FOR HBCU TEACHERS

The Role of the NIH in Graduate Diversity Success

Many graduate institutions have had success in their diversity efforts, which have resulted in measurable outcomes. An important factor in this success has been the support of the National Institutes of Health (NIH). As the primary funding agency for biomedical sciences graduate programs, the NIH has provided key financial support in increasing the number of underrepresented students in pipeline and graduate programs.

The NIH has initiated a number of programs directed primarily at minority-serving institutions to encourage talented students with an interest in science to receive research exposure. These programs, of which the Minority Access to Research Careers (MARC) is an exemplary model, offer some tuition support, a modest stipend, and funding for off-campus summer research.

NIH support has facilitated a dramatic increase in the number of PhDs awarded to underrepresented students in biomedical sciences graduate programs. Additionally, the awarding of training grants is conditioned upon an institution's success in identifying, recruiting, and supporting underrepresented students in the biomedical sciences. Because these grants are highly desired and typically awarded to forward-thinking institutions, the recipient institutions have dramatically increased the number of minority students in the years since the NIH implemented this requirement.

An important factor in this success has been the support of the National Institutes of Health.

Achieving Faculty Diversity

The Case for Minority Faculty Development

Several national studies have linked curricular change, diversity in leadership, institutional commitment, and mission to effectiveness in higher education. Generally, women and minority faculty enhance an institution's ability to achieve the primary missions of research, teaching, and service. Many of the efforts to date have been in medical student diversity. To maximize the benefits of diversity, faculty diversity must also be attended to.

Underrepresented faculty face many challenges that affect their academic productivity. These constraints are a result of institutionalized barriers, time limitations through obligations such as participation on committees, and increased clinical caseloads. Underrepresented faculty often feel pressured to represent their group on every committee while maintaining a teaching role, clinical load, and research productivity, often without the support and mentorship many other faculty enjoy.

Nationally, institutions have provided limited faculty development. In addition, lack of role models and lack of diversity and mentors among senior faculty add barriers to faculty development. In a recent study, underrepresented minority investigators were less likely to be awarded biomedical research funding compared with their white counterparts despite similar scientific achievements.[31] In a published survey, underrepresented minority faculty members were asked to recommend improvements for recruiting and retaining minority faculty. Their responses included a call "for a multifaceted approach to mentorship."[32]

> **A diverse faculty must not only be recruited, but nurtured to succeed.**

Moving forward, it is important to continue to have a strategy for increasing diversity in academic medicine. Supporting underrepresented faculty can attract more underrepresented students to the health professions. A diverse faculty and student body are essential to delivering culturally competent care. Furthermore, faculty play a key role in shaping institutional policies and practices, as well as serving as role models and champions for research on health care disparities. A diverse faculty must not only be recruited, but be nurtured to succeed. It is through their representation and advancement that their voices can result in meaningful change.

In an article making the case for minority faculty development, AAMC Chief Diversity Officer Marc Nivet et al. highlight the following components as areas to address in enhancing an institution's faculty diversity:

- Mentoring Junior Faculty. Mentoring programs significantly enhance the competency of junior faculty.
- Transparency in Promotion and Tenure Guidelines. A common perception of the promotion and tenure process is that it is not always objective. Departments should develop and maintain clearly established criteria for granting promotion and tenure.
- Value Community-Engaged Scholarship (CES). Given that CES is largely engaged in by minority faculty and women, requires a significant amount of time and effort, and builds collaborative skills, it should receive equal consideration in the promotion and tenure process.

- Faculty Development Programs. Departments can develop a variety of programs that assist junior faculty in their development progress.

- Climate of Inclusiveness and Fairness. Professional isolation is often cited as a reason for leaving an institution. Informal social networks can create a sense of community.

- Data Collection. Exit interviews provide the opportunity for understanding obstacles to retention and designing effective responses to problems.

- Self-Assessment. Through regular self-evaluation, departments can avoid disparities in resources and salary that influence faculty retention.

- Flexible Policies and Practices. Flexible family leave, transitional support, work-life balance, and tenure clock policies play key roles in retaining faculty.

Resources

- McDougle L, Lu FG, Castro IL. 2011. Answering the question of the year with faculty diversity. Academic Medicine 86(11):1344.

- Nivet MA et al. 2008. Diversity in academic medicine no. 1 case for minority faculty development today. Mount Sinai Journal of Medicine 75(6):491-498.

Faculty Recruitment

Develop the faculty recruitment plan with a high level of specificity. The most effective search process for diversifying the faculty is conducted in the context of institution-wide commitment to diversity and requires connections outside the standard networks, thoughtful search committee composition, search committee training on unconscious bias, defined standards for candidate evaluation, and a supportive campus climate. Specific guidelines can include the following:

- Descriptions of the position, appointment level, space, and resources need to offer a clear sense of institutional climate.
- The faculty recruitment plan should align with university, school, and departmental missions and goals.
- Data such as residency graduation, regional, and national demographics can help with understanding the available applicant pool.
- Hiring policies should be considered in the context of the university's commitment to diversity and inclusion.
- Current diverse faculty should be engaged as recruiters.
- Diverse recruitment resources should be consulted or developed.
- Search committee composition and training are critical to facilitate a diverse pool of candidates. This includes unconscious bias training for all search committee members.
- Advertisements and calls to colleagues are critical to obtaining a diverse pool.
- A thriving faculty will be your best recruitment tool.
- Include faculty committed to excellence and diversity, women, and individuals from underrepresented groups (ethnic minority, LGBT, those with disabilities) on search committees.

Presidents must hold deans accountable, and deans must hold academic department chairs accountable through performance plans tied to compensation. Based on a department's demographics and applicant pools, specific plans must aim at increasing the representation of women and underrepresented faculty. Some plans may focus on aggressive recruitment from existing pools, and others may focus on building pools if none exist. Here are actions leaders can take to secure a diverse pool of faculty applicants:

- Ensure that funds are available.
- Ensure that the university conducts aggressive, national searches with an emphasis on developing pools that include qualified women and those underrepresented in medicine and biomedical sciences (racial/ethnic minorities, LGBT, those with disabilities) for faculty and administrative positions.
- Require faculty search committee chairs to submit a report about the process used to enhance the pool of qualified candidates and the rationale for inclusion or exclusion in the final pool.
- Require search committee training in unconscious bias.
- Establish a benchmark for excellence in faculty diversity.
- Provide incentives to those who attain the benchmark.

Resources

- Hanson DW. 2010. How to be welcoming. Chronicle of Higher Education.

- University of Michigan Committee on Strategies and Tactics for Recruiting to Improve Diversity and Excellence (STRIDE)

- Hale FW, ed. 2003. What Makes Racial Diversity Work in Higher Education. Sterling, VA: Stylus Publishing. Chapters 12 and 15.

- Bunton SA, Mallon WT. 2007. The continued evolution of faculty appointment and tenure policies at U.S. medical schools. Academic Medicine 82(3):281-89.

- AAMC E-Learning Seminar, What You Don't Know: The Science of Unconscious Bias and What To Do About It in the Search and Recruitment Process

Faculty Development

Unfortunately, even if there is a strong pipeline and recruitment of a diverse faculty, individuals may leave quickly after they are hired, be unable to navigate the tenure process, or be unwilling to stand as the lone representative of their group at their institution. To ensure that all faculty—especially faculty generally underrepresented in medicine or at a specific institution—thrive in their careers, here are a few things to consider:

- **Mentorship.** Formal mentorship is key for underrepresented individuals who often may be the first in their family to attend college and do not have access to a network of support.
- **Individualized Academic Plan.** An individual plan that explores current strengths and skills, future goals, and the path between now and then, is vital for every faculty member. This is particularly true for minority faculty who may be pursuing research in underserved communities or community-engaged scholarship and will need to pursue unique funding sources. A critical aspect of this plan must be a clear timeline for achievement of all the goals therein.
- **Cultural Tax.** Be mindful of the so-called cultural tax. A cultural tax is an obligation felt by minority faculty to be a team player at an institution by serving as a representative for a particular minority group on committees or pursuing opportunities related to being a part of that minority group for the benefit of the institution, even though those pursuits may not fit personal or professional goals.

Celebrate Diversity: Create venues for individuals to socialize and share stories with other minority faculty.

- **Protected Time.** In protecting against a cultural tax or other obligation to the institution, minority faculty need protected time to pursue the goals outlined in their academic plan. Without it, failure is a possibility.
- **Tenure.** If tenure is the goal at an institution, specific requirements and progress toward its attainment must be outlined. Consider an extended tenure clock policy with specific entry requirements for faculty. Policies that also value community-engaged scholarship and nontraditional funding are also vital.
- **Leadership Training and Opportunities.** Outside the tenure process specifically, additional training and opportunities are required to keep faculty engaged.
- **Celebrate Diversity.** Create venues for individuals to socialize and share stories with other minority faculty.

Resources

- Faculty Development for Medical Educators (FD4ME)
- AAMC Minority Faculty Career Development Seminar
- National Institute of Diabetes and Digestive and Kidney Diseases Network of Minority Research Investigators (NMRI)

Achieving Staff Diversity

The staff of an academic medical center are those employees who are not faculty, students, residents, or postdoctoral scholars. They are a critical component of the academic medical center, often serving in administrative and support roles.

The imperative and urgency for diversity of academic medicine staff positions are borne out by the changing U.S. demographics: by 2050, current minority groups will constitute the majority of the U.S. population.[33] Thus, equal attention must be given to the diversity of the institution's administrative, professional, and support staff. Meeting the 21st-century challenges of educating tomorrow's physicians and research scientists requires a workforce that reflects the diversity in the populations being served.

The full benefits of diversity and inclusion are realized when everyone feels valued for contributing to the mission. Creating conditions, policies, and practices that enable the institution to leverage differences toward achieving the mission is the work of inclusion. Diversity councils and affinity network groups that cut across all levels of the institution support inclusion. Typically, these two are the only institutional groups that include membership or representatives from all levels of the system (faculty, staff, students, residents, and postdocs). Their members are stewards of the mission who will ensure a fully inclusive and open environment that provides opportunities for all employees to fully contribute to the institution's success.

The full benefits of diversity and inclusion are realized when everyone feels valued for contributing to the mission.

Part III   References and Resources

References

1   Nivet M. 2011. Diversity 3.0: a necessary systems upgrade. Academic Medicine 86(12): 1487-1489.

2   The Liaison Committee on Medical Education (LCME). 2014. Functions and Structure of a Medical School: Standards for Accreditation of Medical Education Programs Leading to the M.D. Degree. Washington, DC: LCME.

3   Accreditation Council for Graduate Medical Education. 2015. ACGME Common Program Requirements (emphasis added), p. 9.

4   The Joint Commission. 2010. Advancing Effective Communication, Cultural Competence, and Patient-and Family-Centered Care: A Roadmap for Hospitals. Oakbrook Terrace, IL: The Joint Commission. http://www.jointcommission.org/assets/1/6/aroadmapforhospitalsfinalversion727.pdf.

5   The Joint Commission. 2011. Advancing Effective Communication, Cultural Competence, and Patient- and Family-Centered Care for the Lesbian, Gay, Bisexual, and Transgender (LGBT) Community: A Field Guide. OakBrook Terrace, IL: The Joint Commission. http://www.jointcommission.org/assets/1/18/LGBTFieldGuide.pdf.

6   National Conference of State Legislatures (NCSL). 2012. Affirmative Action: State Action. Washington, DC: NCSL. http://www.ncsl.org/issues-research/educ/affirmative-action- state-action.aspx.

7   Grutter v. Bollinger. 539 U.S. 306, 123 S. Ct. 2325, 156 L. Ed. 2d 304 (2003).

8   Fisher v. University of Texas at Austin. 570 U.S. 391, 133 S. Ct. 2411, 186 L. Ed. 2d 474 (2013).

9   The Sullivan Commission. 2004. Missing Persons: Minorities in the Health Professions—A Report of the Sullivan Commission on Diversity in the Healthcare Workforce. Washington, DC: Sullivan Commission. http://depts.washington.edu/ccph/pdf_files/Sullivan_Report_ES.pdf.

10 James J. 2012. Health Policy Brief: pay-for-performance. Health Affairs. http://www.healthaffairs.org/healthpolicybriefs/brief.php?brief_id=78.

11 Dartmouth Atlas Project. 2013. The Revolving Door: A Report on U.S. Hospital Readmissions. Princeton, NJ: Robert Wood Johnson Foundation. http://www.rwjf.org/content/ dam/farm/reports/reports/2013/rwjf404178.

12 Center for Disease Control and Prevention. 2013. CDC health disparities & inequalities report (CHDIR). http://www.cdc.gov/minorityhealth/CHDIReport.html.

13 United States Census Bureau. 2012. Most children younger than age 1 are minorities, Census Bureau reports. http://www. census.gov/newsroom/releases/archives/population/cb12-90.html.

14 Lupton K, Vercammen-Grandjean C, Forkin J, Wilson E, Grumbach K. 2012. Specialty choice and practice location of physician alumni of University of California premedical postbaccalaureate programs. Academic Medicine 87(1):115-120.

15   Saha S, Guiton G, Wimmers P F, Wilkerson L. 2008. Student body racial and ethnic composition and diversity-related outcomes in US medical schools. JAMA 300(10):1135-1145.

16   Antonio AL, Chang MJ, Hakuta K, Kenny DA, Levin S, Milem J F. 2004. Effects of racial diversity on complex thinking in college students. Psychological Science 15(8):507-510.

17   Whitla DK, Orfield G, Silen W, Teperow C, Howard C, Reede J. 2003). Educational benefits of diversity in medical school: a survey of students. Academic Medicine 78(5):460-466.

18   Hurtado S. 2005. The next generation of diversity and intergroup relations research. Journal of Social Issues 61(3):595-610.

19   Saha S, Guiton G, Wimmers PF, Wilkerson L. 2008. Student body racial and ethnic composition and diversity-related outcomes in US medical schools. JAMA 300(10):1135-1145.

20   Chang MJ, Denson N, Saenz V, Misa K. 2006. The educational benefits of sustaining cross-racial interaction among undergraduates. Journal of Higher Education 77(3):430-455.

21   Committee on Underrepresented Groups and the Expansion of the Science and Engineering Workforce Pipeline et al. 2010. Expanding Underrepresented Minority Participation: America's Science and Technology Talent at the Crossroads. Washington, DC: National Academies Press.

22   Committee on Equal Opportunities in Science and Engineering. 2013. 2011–2012 Biennial Report to Congress: Broadening Participation in America's STEM Workforce. Arlington, VA: National Science Foundation.

23   Swing SR. 2007. The ACGME outcome project: retrospective and prospective. Medical Teacher 29(7):648-654.

24   Kearney E, Gebert D. 2009. Managing diversity and enhancing team outcomes: the promise of transformational leadership. Journal of Applied Psychology 94(1):77-89.

25   The Accreditation Council for Graduate Medical Education (ACGME). http://www.acgme.org/acgmeweb/.

26   For an example, see Figure 1 in Rose SH, Long TR. 2010. Accreditation Council for Graduate Medical Education (ACGME) annual anesthesiology residency and fellowship program review. BMC Medical Education 10(13). http://biomedcentral.com/1472-6920/10/13.

27   Chin JL. 2010. Introduction to the special issue on diversity and leadership. American Psychologist 65(3):150-156.

28   U.S. Census Bureau. 2011. Overview of Race and Hispanic Origin: 2010.https://www.census.gov/prod/cen2010/briefs/c2010br-02.pdf.

29   National Center for Science and Engineering Statistics. 2013. Women, Minorities, and Persons with Disabilities in Science and Engineering: 2013. Arlington, VA: National Science Foundation.

30   Garrison H. 2013. Underrepresentation by race–ethnicity across stages of U.S. science and engineering education. CBE Life Sciences Education 12(3):357-363.

31   Ginther DK et al. 2011. Race, ethnicity, and NIH research awards. Science 333(6045):1015-1019.

32   Mahoney MR et al. 2008. Minority faculty voices on diversity in academic medicine: perspective from one school. Academic Medicine 83(8):781-786.

33   Passel JS, Cohn D. 2008. U.S. Population Projections: 2005–2050. Washington, DC: Pew Research Center.

Additional Strategic Planning Resources

The following references on the overall strategic planning process offer a deeper look into many of the subjects discussed in this guide.

Barry BW. 1998. A beginner's guide to strategic planning. The Futurist 32(3):33-36.

Becker BN, Formisano RA. 2006. Strategic planning for departmental divisions in an academic health care center. American Journal of Medicine 119(4):357-365.

Bonazza J, Farrell PM, Albanese M, Kindig D. 2000. Collaboration and peer review in medical schools' strategic planning. Academic Medicine 75(5): 409-418.

Briggs S, Keogh W. 1999. Integrating human resource strategy and strategic planning to achieve business excellence. Total Quality Management 10(4/5):S447-S453.

Cook DC, Nelson E-L, Ast C, Lillis T. 2013. A systematic strategic planning process focused on improved community engagement by an academic health center: the University of Kansas Medical Center's story. Academic Medicine 88(5):614-619.

Deas D, Pisano ED, Mainous AG, Johnson NG, Singleton MH, Gordon L et al. 2012. Improving diversity through strategic planning: a 10-year (2002–2012) experience at the Medical University of South Carolina. Academic Medicine 87(11):1548-1555.

Dye R, Sibony O. 2007. How to improve strategic planning. McKinsey Quarterly 3(40).

Walters EW, McKay S. 2005. Strategic planning and retention within the community college setting. College Student Affairs Journal 25(1):50-63.

Fogg CD. 1998. Implementing Your Strategic Plan How to Turn "Intent" into Effective Action for Sustainable Change. New York: AMACOM.

Galunic C. Hermreck I. 2012. How to help employees "get" strategy. Harvard Business Review 90(12):24-24.

Giffords ED, Dina RP. 2004. Strategic planning in nonprofit organizations: continuous quality performance improvement—a case study. International Journal of Organization Theory and Behavior 7(1):66-80.

Gordon J, Hazlett C, Cate O, Mann K, Kilminster S, Prince K, Newble D. 2000. Strategic planning in medical education: enhancing the learning environment for students in clinical settings. Medical Education 34(10):841-850.

Hambrick DC, Fredrickson JW. 2001. Are you sure you have a strategy? Academy of Management Executive 15(4):48-59.

Harmon RB, Fontaine D, Plews-Ogan M, Williams A. 2012. Achieving transformational change: using appreciative inquiry for strategic planning in a school of nursing. Journal of Professional Nursing 28(2):119-124.

Hazlett JA, Carayannis EG. 1998. Business-university virtual teaming for strategic planning. Technological Forecasting and Social Change 57(3):261-265.

Hill SEK, Thomas EG, Keller LF. 2009. A collaborative, ongoing university strategic planning framework: process, landmines, and lessons. Planning for Higher Education 37(4):16-26.

Jennings D, Disney JJ. 2006. Designing the strategic planning process: does psychological type matter? Management Decision 44(5):598-614.

Johnson RD, Lipp A. 2007. Cognitive mapping: a process to support strategic planning in an academic department. Group Decision and Negotiation 16(1):43-60.

Kaplan RS, Norton DP. 2008. Mastering the management system. Harvard Business Review 86(1):62-77.

Kaplan RS, Norton DP. 2001. The Strategy-Focused Organization: How Balanced Scorecard Companies Thrive in the New Business Environment. Boston, MA: Harvard Business School Press.

Kola IM, Selesho JM. 2012. The role of the academic heads of departments in the strategic planning of the university. Anthropologist 14(3):209-214.

Levinson W, Axler H. 2007. Strategic planning in a complex academic environment: lessons from one academic health center. Academic Medicine 82(8):806-811.

Miech EJ. 1995. Editor's review. Harvard Educational Review 65(3):504.

Mintzberg H. 1994. The Rise and Fall of Strategic Planning: Reconceiving Roles For Planning, Plans, Planners. New York: Free Press.

Moxley DP. 2004. Factors influencing the successful use of vision-based strategy planning by nonprofit human service organizations. International Journal of Organization Theory and Behavior 7(1):107-132.

Nauffal DI, Nasser RN. 2012. Strategic planning at two levels. Planning for Higher Education 40(4):32-39.

Porter ME. 1996. What is strategy? Harvard Business Review 74(6):61.

Rumelt R. 2011. The perils of bad strategy. McKinsey Quarterly 1:30-39.

Schmidt C. 2013. Strategic planning for future learning environments: an exploration of interpersonal, interprofessional, and political factors. Journal of Interprofessional Care 27:46-50.

Sokol R. 1992. Simplifying strategic planning. Management Decision 30(7):11.

Thompson ME, Harver A, Eure M. 2009. A model for integrating strategic planning and competence-based curriculum design in establishing a public health programme: the UNC Charlotte experience. Human Resources for Health 7(71).

Tucker P. 2007. A handbook for scenario planning. The Futurist 41(2):50.

Weitekamp MR, Thorndyke LE, Evarts CM. 1996. Strategic planning for academic health centers. American Journal of Medicine 101(3):309-315.

Welsh JF, Nunez WJ, Petrosko J. 2005. Faculty and administrative support for strategic planning: a comparison of two- and four-year institutions. Community College Review 32(4):20-39.

DATE DUE

8/31	
1/08	

DEMCO, INC. 38-2931

Made in the USA
Lexington, KY
07 April 2017